Rituals
for Beginners

About the Author

Richard Webster is the author of more than fifty titles with Llewellyn, and he is one of New Zealand's most prolific writers. His best-selling books include *Face Reading Quick & Easy*, *Spirit Guides and Angel Guardians*, *Miracles*, and a series of books on feng shui. MagicNZ presented him with a Lifetime Achievement Award for "excellence in writing magical literature" in 2008. His book *Spirit and Dream Animals* received a COVR Award in 2012. In 2013, Richard was made a Grand Master of Magic by the magicians of New Zealand. He has appeared on numerous TV shows including *Hard Copy* and *20/20*. His books have been translated into thirty-one languages.

Rituals

for Beginners

Simple Ways to Connect to Your Spiritual Side

Richard Webster

Llewellyn Publications
Woodbury, Minnesota

FIRST EDITION
First Printing, 2016

Cover art: istockphoto.com/21682429/KovacsAlex
Cover design: Ellen Lawson
Edited by: Stephanie Finne

Llewellyn Publications is a registered trademark of Llewellyn Worldwide Ltd.

Library of Congress Cataloging-in-Publication Data
Webster, Richard, 1946–
  Rituals for beginners : simple ways to connect to your spiritual side / by Richard Webster. — FIRST EDITION.
    pages cm
  ISBN 978-0-7387-4765-1
  1. Rites and ceremonies. 2. Ritualism. 3. Ritual. I. Title.
  BL600.W425 2016
  203'.8—dc23
                                                        2015015229

Llewellyn Publications
A Division of Llewellyn Worldwide Ltd.
2143 Wooddale Drive
Woodbury, MN 55125-2989
www.llewellyn.com

Printed in the United States of America

Other Books by Richard Webster

contents

rituals list

introduction

Not long ago I surprised a friend by telling him his regular habit of going bowling every Wednesday evening was a ritual. He thought rituals were conducted in a house of worship, and he found it hard to believe that even something like shaking hands or saying "thank you" could be considered a ritual.

By definition, a ritual is an action, or series of actions, performed in a prearranged, prescribed manner. Anything that follows a set pattern could be described as a ritual. Even the process of getting out of bed and preparing for work could be called a ritual, as most people perform the necessary actions in the same way every day. Saying grace before a meal is a form of ritual as is blowing out the candles on a birthday cake. My daily walk is a form of ritual. My grandchildren love hanging up their Christmas stockings. This is also a ritual.

I worked as an entertainer for many years, and, consequently, my wife and I never went out together on a Saturday night. Because of that, we now go to a movie or a show every Saturday night, and it's become a ritual. Every Sunday evening, our children and grandchildren come to our home for dinner. That's my favorite ritual. Thanksgiving, bridal showers, knocking on wood, avoiding walking under a ladder, or tossing a pinch of salt over your shoulder are all ritualistic acts.

Rituals are often associated with religious ceremonies. A religious ritual is a formal, well-defined, spiritual experience. The intention of a religious ritual is to bring people closer to God. Taking Holy Communion or attending a Catholic Mass are good examples of this type of ritual. The prayers, invocations, singing of hymns, and the special clothing and equipment worn and used by priests all add to the power and effectiveness of the ritual. Religious rituals help people connect to something greater than themselves and enable them to experience the spiritual side of their nature.

As a child I went to a church school and, like all the other pupils, attended a variety of services and ceremonies. However, I did this purely because it was expected of me. I said the required responses, but I did it purely by rote. Although I enjoyed some aspects of these services, especially the singing in the chapel, they all seemed a waste of time. Because I was never taught the meaning of these rituals, they meant nothing to me. It took me many years to learn that rituals were an important way to achieve spiritual transformation.

For thousands of years, rituals have been associated with the important transitions and milestones of life, such as birth, christening, puberty, marriage, parenthood, and death. Rituals still play an important part in these transitions, as they support, encourage, and assist our progress from one stage to the next.

We all have small rituals that help us handle life. These rituals have a beneficial effect on our mental and physical health. Rituals help us control stress and can, in fact, keep us sane. Pausing for a cup of coffee or a chat with a friend are rituals that help us cope with all the minor irritations that life sends our way. Of course, some rituals, such as drinking to excess or indulging in too much "retail therapy," can produce more problems than they solve. Consequently, we need to ensure that our small daily rituals are beneficial rather than harmful.

Rituals are conducted for many purposes. There are four essential ingredients that are necessary to make the ritual effective: importance, intention, mindfulness, and sacred space.

Importance

To be effective, the ritual must have meaning to you. Many people find personal meaning in attending, say, a church service. They find importance and meaning in participating in a ritual that has been performed in much the same way for hundreds, or thousands, of years. Other people attending the same service may get nothing from the service. They may sing the hymns and say the correct responses, but if they attach no importance to what they're doing, the personal meaning and power is lost.

Intention

There is an intention, or purpose, behind every ritual. When I set out on my daily walk, my intention is to have time on my own to think. Naturally, I'm doing it partly for exercise, but the main purpose is to get out in the fresh air and reflect on what is going on in my life. The ritual starts when I put on my sneakers, and finishes after I've had a glass of water on my return home.

Dion Fortune, the British occultist and author, wrote that "any act performed with intention becomes a rite." She used the example of taking a bath. If the bath was taken solely for physical cleanliness, that's all it would be. However, it was undertaken with the intention of "ritual cleanliness," it would accomplish much more (Fortune 1970).

Mindfulness

It's important to remain in the moment when performing a ritual. Rituals keep us centered and focused on what we're doing. It's impossible to worry about day-to-day problems while taking part in a ritual. Rituals force us to slow down and live in the present moment.

Sacred Space

All religions have a sacred space, known as a *temenos*, which is separated from the everyday world. Christians, for instance, have churches, Jews have synagogues, and Hindus have temples. *Temenos* is a Greek word that means "a sanctuary or place that is dedicated to the gods."

It's helpful to create the right environment for your rituals by performing them in a designated area. This sets them apart from your normal life and emphasizes their importance. When I go for a walk, my sacred space is the sidewalk I walk along. Our home becomes my sacred space when the family comes for dinner.

You can create a sacred space anywhere you wish. You might use candles and crystals to mark out your sacred space, or you might simply imagine a circle surrounding you. Some people enjoy a leisurely bath before starting a ritual. This also serves to separate the ritual from their daily lives. In fact, a bath can be a ritual in itself, if the intention is purification.

The purpose of this book is to help you understand the power of ritual and to encourage you to make use of it to enhance your own life.

We all perform ritualistic actions on a regular basis, even if it is as simple as buying a newspaper from the same store every morning. Usually, these rituals are not planned and begin without any conscious intention. However, many people perform ritualistic actions consciously and deliberately. Members of the clergy do this whenever they conduct a service. They help people find spiritual meaning. Many Pagans, Wiccans, and magicians also use rituals to help them achieve their goals. This is known as ritual magic. Rituals that are performed consciously provide calmness and serenity in the midst of the hectic lives most of us lead.

one

How Rituals Can Enhance Your Life

Rituals provide many benefits, all of which have the potential to enhance your life in many ways. Here are some of the most important ones.

- Rituals provide confidence and peace of mind.
- Rituals enable you to perform tasks more quickly and efficiently.
- Rituals enable you to ease yourself into performing tasks that aren't exciting.
- Rituals help you establish closer relationships.
- Rituals make you appreciate things more than before.
- Rituals can help you release emotion.

- Rituals provide stability.
- Rituals at the start and end of the day provide contentment and peace of mind.
- Rituals strengthen your connection with the divine.
- Rituals help you appreciate life.

Let's briefly look at these. Rituals provide confidence and peace of mind as they put you in control. Performing a ritual, no matter what it is, enables you to do something that makes you feel better about whatever it is you need to do. People who play competitive sports are well aware of this.

While preparing for a game, Michael Jordan always put on his North Carolina shorts before putting on his Chicago Bulls shorts. Wade Boggs, who used to play for the Boston Red Sox, did much more than that. He woke up at the same time every morning, and he always ate chicken before playing a game. He also took exactly 117 ground balls during practice, started batting practice at exactly 5:17 p.m., and ran sprints at 7:17 p.m. Before each turn at bat, he wrote the Hebrew word *Chai* (meaning "living") in the ground (Gino and Norton 2013). These might seem like superstitions, but these rituals made them feel more confident, and because of this they enjoyed peace of mind and played better as a result.

Rituals enable you to perform tasks more quickly and efficiently as they enable you to get straight into the task without the need to invest time beforehand. My mother always enjoyed a cup of coffee before putting the washing on the clothesline. Once she'd finished her coffee, she immediately got up and, without even thinking about it, hung up the clothes to dry.

I do something similar when I'm outlining a book. I make myself a pot of green tea and immediately sit down and start writing my thoughts on the new project.

A friend of mine sits down in a comfortable chair, closes his eyes, and takes a few slow, deep breaths. He then thinks about the task he's about to do and how good he'll feel when it's completed. He enjoys the visualization, and he finds it motivates him to action.

Rituals provide a way to ease yourself into performing tasks that don't excite you. I have an exercise program that I should perform every other day. However, because I'm not always excited about exercise, I skip a day here and there, and before I know it my exercise program is almost nonexistent. I created a small ritual that motivates me to stick to my program. On the days when I'm going to exercise, before getting out of bed I tell myself, with as much enthusiasm as I can, "Today's the day when I get to exercise!" This works like magic. I immediately feel excited about the upcoming exercise, and am motivated and ready to start my workout. I learned this technique from an opera singer I heard interviewed on the radio many years ago. The interviewer said, "Poor you. You've got to go and work tonight." The opera singer replied, "Oh, no. Tonight I get to sing!"

Of course, your ritual can be anything at all. It might be having a cup of tea or coffee or maybe listening to a favorite piece of music. Once you've performed the ritual, you'll find yourself automatically moving on to the task you have to do.

A friend told me that performing a brief ritual frees up his mind, as he doesn't need to think about the task he's about to undertake. Rituals of this sort soon become habits, and you'll find yourself working your way through all the unexciting tasks without any procrastination or delaying tactics.

Rituals enable you to establish closer relationships with family and friends. For some unknown reason, Sunday seems to be my day for rituals of this sort. Every Sunday morning I meet a group of friends at a local café for coffee and a chat. We spend about two hours discussing movies, sports, and current events. It has become a valuable ritual, as it enables me to see some of my best friends every week.

As I mentioned earlier, my favorite ritual is having our children and grandchildren visit us on Sunday night for dinner. Every couple of months I meet my brother and sister for lunch. This is another family ritual that I look forward to. We'd get together more often than that, but because all of us travel frequently, we're not able to see each other as often as we'd wish.

The advantages of rituals of this sort are that they enable you to establish closer and deeper relationships with the special people in your life. They increase a sense of belonging, and this increases feelings of security and comfort.

Rituals make you appreciate things more than before. Researchers have discovered that employees who perform rituals as part of their work experience greater job satisfaction, and consumers who perform a ritual to try out a new product enjoy it more and are prepared to pay more for it (Halverson 2013). There are many examples of this. Many people know the Oreo cookie ritual (twist it, lick it, dunk it). Nespresso treats customers like royalty in their stores while demonstrating their coffee machines. Guinness stout has to be poured at an angle and allowed to settle for two minutes before the rest of the pint is added. If you have a product to sell, try adding a ritual to it, as chances are people will buy more of what you have to offer.

Rituals can help you release emotion. You can take part in a parade or a presentation for someone who has achieved something worthwhile. You can participate in a ritual where two people you care about get married. You can also attend a funeral service and grieve for someone you cared about. Sharing the emotion with others is an excellent way to release it.

You can also release emotions privately. When someone I used to work with was dumped by her boyfriend, she created a small ritual in which she burned all his love letters to her. She told me she found it cathartic, and it enabled her to let go of the past and start looking forward again.

Rituals provide stability to your life. Anything you do on a regular basis provides comfort and reassurance. You may have a number of these. You might, for instance, go for a brisk walk with a friend every Monday evening. On Wednesdays you might go bowling with friends. On Fridays you and your family might enjoy a pizza night. The regular reoccurrence of these small rituals provides pleasure and something to look forward to every week.

Rituals at the start and end of the day provide contentment and peace of mind. Many people feel they are too busy to perform a ritual first thing in the morning. However, morning rituals can be something as small as doing a few stretching exercises, drinking a glass of water or a cup of coffee, brushing your teeth, checking e-mails, or reading the morning paper. A friend of mine is learning Spanish by studying it for ten minutes every morning. It has become a ritual that he's finding increasingly useful as he can now enjoy conversations with his Hispanic neighbors in their own language.

A manager at a company I worked for when I was a teenager started each day by looking at himself in his bathroom mirror and saying "Boy, I'm enthusiastic!" three times. He increased the volume and intensity each time he repeated the phrase. As he was one of the most enthusiastic people I've ever met, this ritual paid big dividends for him.

It's usually easier to create a ritual to mark the end of the day. My bedtime ritual is to read for about ten minutes when I get in bed. This enables me to relax, and I fall asleep almost as soon as I turn out the light. A lady I know enjoys spending several minutes alone in her garden before going to bed. She does this even in the middle of winter. I know several people who write in a journal before going to bed.

Experiment with a few rituals at the start and the end of the day. Once you've found something you enjoy, do it regularly until it becomes a habit. You'll find these small rituals will provide pleasure as well as contentment.

Rituals can also increase your connection with the divine. Spiritual rituals can be performed at any time, wherever you happen to be. You don't need incense or an altar. A prayer or even the recitation of a spiritual poem are good examples of spiritual rituals. A friend of mine silently sends thoughts of love to everyone he sees when he's out and about.

Many years ago, we had a neighbor who got rid of the stresses and pressures he'd picked up during the day by vigorously shaking himself while standing outside his front door. It looked as if he was doing a strange type of dance. While doing this, he'd make a silent prayer of thanks for all the positive aspects of his life. Once he felt he'd shaken away all of the negativity he'd picked up during the day, he'd open his front door and walk inside.

Rituals help you appreciate life. Most rituals involve an element of gratitude that enables you to express your thanks for all of your life's blessings. All of us take most of these blessings for granted. You're unlikely to think about the blessing of good health, for instance, until you become sick. Most people are too busy to even think about giving thanks. Fortunately, you can include gratitude in any ritual you perform. Doing this makes you feel good. More importantly, you'll find that this helps you become more patient and tolerant in everyday life.

As you can see, there are many benefits from performing rituals large and small. In the next chapter, we'll look at some of the more important rituals that we experience as we progress through life.

two

Rituals of Life

Rituals are often performed to indicate the important transition stages of life. This is because we all have a deep need to mark important rites of passage. Many religions conduct rituals to mark the important transitions of birth, marriage, and death. However, there are many other occasions throughout life that deserve to be commemorated. These include: naming or baptism, puberty, becoming a teenager, leaving home, engagement, uncoupling or divorce, educational and career accomplishments, promotion, recognition from the community, menopause, recovery from illness, and retirement. It's also important to celebrate regular milestones, such as birthdays and the New Year.

All of these occasions occur when a person has completed one stage of life and is about to start another. When a person completes a degree and enters the workforce, he or she has finished formal education (at least for the moment) and embarked on a career. When a friend of mine recovered from a serious illness, he ceased being sick and became well again. A young man I know recently obtained his driver's license. This is an important turning point in his life, as it is a major step toward full independence.

All of these stages, or turning points, deserve to be recognized. My parents celebrated all important transitions with a special meal and a glass of wine. My brother, sisters, and I were given a watered-down glass of wine on these occasions. At some stage during the meal, my father would propose a toast to whatever it was we were celebrating. It wasn't until many years later that I understood this family tradition was an important ritual that marked all of the important events in our lives. This ritual wasn't structured, but I'm sure my parents discussed it and made arrangements for it ahead of time.

Rituals of life can be as formal or as casual as you wish. As with all rituals, the most important part is the intent behind it.

Pregnancy

It's an exciting moment when a couple discovers that they're going to have a child. Some people like to celebrate this momentous news immediately, while others prefer to wait until the second or third trimester. The couple might like to do something together to celebrate the pregnancy. They might have a small occasion that includes family and close friends, or they might celebrate with a large party.

Recently my wife and I attended a party to celebrate a pregnancy. A forty-two-year-old woman my wife works with had become pregnant after several anxious years where she'd been unable to conceive. Because of this, they wanted to hold a big party and invite almost everyone they knew. It was an extremely happy occasion, though there were a few tears as my wife's friend told us exactly what she'd been through and how this was probably going to be their one and only child.

The couple had created a charming ritual for the occasion. After the speeches, they sat down together with their arms around each other. The guests all lined up, came up to the couple, gently touched her obviously pregnant abdomen, and said a few words to the unborn baby.

Pre-Birth

Pre-birth rituals are comparatively new. Baby showers are a charming ritual that began with the baby boomers after World War II.

It's becoming increasingly common for people to hold a pre-birth ritual to commemorate the imminent arrival of new life. Usually, this is done as part of a small party where the parents-to-be invite their friends and relatives to attend. In the past, women usually attended pre-birth celebrations, but today men are just as welcome as the women.

Birth

Ideally, the birth of a child is a joyous occasion for the whole family. When the birth is a happy one for everyone involved, family and friends will visit to see the new arrival and to congratulate the proud parents. It's traditional to bring a gift and to have something to eat and drink with the proud parents.

Naming

In the past, most people in Christian countries had their babies baptized in a church. This service made the child a member of the Christian Church and also told the world what his or her name was. Other religions had their own versions of this. In Hinduism, for instance, the baby is named eleven days after birth. In Islam, the child is named seven days after birth. In Judaism, boys are named eight days after birth, and girls are named when the father is called up to the Torah on the closest Torah Reading Day to the girl's birth.

Nowadays, many people perform their own naming rituals. Some of these are performed by celebrants, but frequently the parents hold their own rites in which the newly named child is shown to close friends and family.

Adoption

A few years ago, my wife and I attended a small party that friends put on to welcome an adopted child into their family. Because the child was seven years old and knew what was going on, she played a major role in the ritual.

Once everyone had arrived, the couple told everyone of the special event that had happened in their lives and asked everyone to say a big hello to their new daughter. The little girl enjoyed this, and she waved a hand and said hello to the guests. She then hugged her new parents and told them how much she loved them. After this she read a short poem that she'd written that told how she'd longed for a mother and a father and how thrilled she was to finally have parents. It was a moving ritual that everyone present will remember.

Puberty

Puberty marks the change from childhood to adolescence. The marked physical and psychological changes that occur at this stage can make it difficult to create a specific ritual to mark the occasion. If the young person is willing, a party could be held in which the special people in his or her life are invited to help celebrate this major milestone. One or two people could be invited to speak about the young person's childhood and how he or she is entering adolescence, with more responsibilities and choices as he or she progresses toward adulthood.

Alternatively, the occasion could be celebrated with a family meal in which the young person gets to choose what will be served.

Leaving Home

It's a momentous occasion in a young person's life when he or she leaves home for the first time. This is often an exciting occasion for the young person concerned, but it can leave a large gap in the lives of the people left behind. It's important that this significant milestone is marked in some way, and that the parting is made as smooth as possible for everyone concerned.

Turning Twenty-One

Turning twenty-one is a significant milestone, even though today most young adults are already enjoying all the privileges that adulthood confers on them well before they reach this age. This celebration is often marked by a party containing small rituals that many adults present don't fully approve of but remember doing themselves when they were twenty-one.

Engagement

Proposing marriage is an extremely important ritual, and it's one where tradition still plays a role. Traditionally, the man proposes to the woman. He's also likely to get down on one knee to propose. This is followed by the presentation of an engagement ring that tells the world the exciting news. The announcement of the couple's engagement can be made in many ways, but it is often made at a party put on by the bride-to-be's parents.

Handfasting/Marriage

Many people nowadays choose not to have a traditional church wedding, or even have a wedding at all. However, even if a wedding only lasts a few minutes in a registry office, it's still a ritual that joins the bride and groom together at a sacred, divine level. Wiccans call their wedding vows "handfasting." A handfasting may be for "a year and a day," which is, in effect, a trial marriage, or (hopefully) for life. If a couple marries for a year and a day, the partners can make the relationship permanent at the end of that time, or if they decide the relationship is not working, go their separate ways.

Uncoupling, Separation, and Divorce

Unfortunately, not all relationships last and a large percentage end in divorce. This is painful for everyone involved, and some people feel regrets about the failed relationship for many years after it has ended. Consequently, a ritual that marks the end of the relationship can help everyone let go and move on. It's beneficial if both former partners can attend the ritual, but it's more common for only one to be present. At the ritual, someone should talk about the positive aspects of the relationship as well as the negative. This is often best done by a friend of the former bride or groom who can speak about the relationship without emotion. Ideally, this ritual should be performed in a place that has no special memories for either party.

Retirement

Entering retirement used to mean that the person had finished his or her significant life and was effectively waiting to die. Fortunately, this is no longer the case. Many people who are well beyond traditional retirement age are still working, and the ones who are retired are often active in their community, traveling, pursuing hobbies and interests, and generally leading full, satisfying, and enjoyable lives.

When my grandfather retired, the company he worked for put on a small party to say farewell. Everyone drank sherry, and he was presented with a rather ugly clock. Fifty or sixty years ago, that was the sort of ritual that marked this particular change in life.

Many people enter retirement with a number of fears. They worry about their future health, wonder if their money will last long enough, and hope they won't be a burden to their family. Consequently, entering retirement can be a stressful time for many people.

A suitable ritual can help allay these fears and enable the new retiree to see that the future is full of opportunities that they didn't have before. They have the ability to create a lifestyle that suits them. They'll have time to do things they'd always dreamed about, and so on.

Recently, I attended a retirement party for an attorney. He gave a highly entertaining talk on how happy he was to leave the legal profession behind because he had a long list of things he intended to do before he died. It took him about ten minutes to tell us what they all were. This man considered retirement to be the start of a whole new life. His party was a ritual to mark the end of one stage of his life and the start of the next.

Health

It's a rare and lucky person who lives a long life without any major health issues along the way. If you or anyone close to you needs medical care, consider holding a special ritual to enable friends to express their love and support. This ritual is beneficial for everyone involved, and it appears to speed up the healing process.

Rituals of this sort should be done both before and after any medical procedures.

Death

Along with taxes, death is the only thing we can completely count on. Formal Christian and Jewish funerals are rituals that give hope and comfort to many people. In fact, research shows that believers and nonbelievers alike receive comfort from funeral rituals as they provide a sense of being in control (Jarrett 2013).

This applies even for people who believe in reincarnation. For them, death is simply a transitional stage where the person goes until it is time to be born again. A special ritual that enables the mourners to grieve and yet be happy that the person is reconnecting with the universal life force before being born again can be extremely comforting and helpful for the person's loved ones.

In addition to the funeral, it can be highly therapeutic for the family and close friends of the deceased to be able to spend time together talking about the person's life. This could be considered a ritual of healing and comfort.

Several years ago, the family of a good friend of mine who had died put on an afternoon tea to display his artwork and to share memories. We all enjoyed listening to the stories and contributing stories of our own. As my friend had been about to start a retirement career as an artist, it was a wonderful opportunity to see examples of his paintings and appreciate the high quality of work he was producing. Several people told me afterward how beneficial and helpful this afternoon tea ritual had been.

New Beginnings

There are many times in life when people have to make a new start. Common examples include breakups, divorces, death of loved ones, starting life again after a serious illness, moving to a new town or even country, and starting a new job or career. Even though some of these are happy new starts, all of them are likely to be stressful. Holding a ritual to let go of the past and to welcome in a new way of life can ease the stress.

Family Rituals

Most families have rituals of one sort or another. They may not be called rituals, but that is what they are. Birthdays, promotions at work, exam and sporting successes, a move to a new home, and any other family celebrations can all be celebrated with a ritual.

A friend of mine established a Christmas ritual for his family many years ago. Every member of the family receives a strange or unusual gift along with a letter from "Uncle Albert" that tells them about his adventures and travels to exotic destinations around the world and how he hopes to see them next Christmas. Of course, he never does. My friend came up with the idea of an imaginary uncle when his children were small. He is now a grandfather, and he is constantly looking for unusual and inexpensive gifts for "Uncle Albert" to give to his ever-growing family.

Death of a Pet

A number of people have told me they cried more when a much-loved pet died than when a relative passed over. This is not surprising when you think of the time and emotion people invest in their pets. The loss of a pet can be heart-breaking, and a suitable ritual can help people handle the grief process.

Not long ago my grandchildren's cat died. He was a highly social Burmese cat that enjoyed playing with the children and always participated in family gatherings. We all loved him. Unfortunately, he developed liver cancer, and he died two days after being taken to the veterinarian.

The children were devastated, and their father created a ritual that helped them handle their grief. The family all sat around the kitchen table. They lit a white candle and everyone took a turn to say what Coco had meant to him or her. They told funny stories about different things he'd done and how they loved it when he chose their bed to sleep on. They finished the ritual by holding hands and saying a prayer. The time spent talking about their loss proved helpful for everyone, and it enabled them to start moving forward again.

The loss of a pet doesn't necessarily mean it has died. There have been many instances in the media about celebrity couples breaking up and fighting over who keeps the family pet. This is understandable, as the unconditional love and devotion of a pet is even more valuable than usual in the midst of a relationship breakup. This is why the family pet can become a weapon when two people are fighting. In cases of this sort, a ritual can be extremely helpful. It gives the person the opportunity to thank the pet for its love and devotion and to wish it well in the future.

Rituals After a Traumatic Event

Unfortunately, many people suffer from the aftereffects of violence and abuse. Victims of rape and childhood sexual abuse can suffer for the rest of their lives if they can't come to terms with what happened and release the pain and anguish. A ritual that enables them to forgive the perpetrator without condoning what has been done, let go of the trauma, and look ahead again can do a great deal to help people handle what has been done to them.

Obviously, a ritual of this sort can only be performed when the victim is ready to let go of what happened. About twenty years ago, I received a phone call from a friend I'd known since childhood inviting me to attend a small ritual. He didn't tell me any more over the phone, and I was surprised to learn at the ritual that he'd been sexually abused as a child. Even though we were good friends throughout our childhood, he'd never given me as much as the slightest hint about what had been going on. During the ritual he said, "I've got to let go of this. It hurts too much, and if I don't let it go it will kill me." None of his friends or family had any idea about the suffering and anguish he'd experienced.

The ritual was simple. All the guests were given a glass of wine to hold, and we stood in a circle around him and listened while he told us what had happened thirty years earlier. When he finished, he asked us to raise our glasses and have a toast "to the future." To this day, my friend refuses to discuss what happened to him, but he's noticeably a much happier, far more relaxed person. He's also much more affectionate. Because a ritual of this sort can be highly emotional, it needs to be handled sensitively with people the victim loves and trusts.

three

Everyday Rituals

We all have rituals that we perform every day. Getting out of bed, our commute to work, the people we interact with at work, and relaxing in the evening before going to bed are all ritualistic acts that place a sense of order on our lives. In addition to these, there are other rituals that can be performed whenever necessary to help make our lives smoother, happier, and easier.

Most people lead busy lives, and they seldom pause to nurture themselves. I'm sure many physical problems, such as headaches and backaches, would disappear if everyone gave themselves a few precious minutes every day to relax and perform a small ritual.

Hannah, an acquaintance of mine, was on medication to help her control stress when she discovered the benefits of regular everyday rituals.

"I never had any time for myself," she told me. "I'm bringing up three children on my own, and I'm constantly attending to the needs of others. My doctor prescribed medications for stress and anxiety. However, I no longer need them, as three times a day, I take a few minutes for myself. I'm amazed that spending less than ten minutes a day on myself is enough to change my life."

Hannah's rituals are extremely simple. She prays twice a day, focusing on giving thanks for the blessings in her life. Before going to bed at night, she writes in her journal.

"I try to write mainly positive things," she told me. "Every day I expect good things to happen, and I'm always looking for them. I write them all down in my journal. I've had some terrible days, but every night I find at least one good thing to write down."

Hannah's intention is to be grateful for all the blessings in her life. Because she takes a few minutes, three times a day, to think about all the good things in her life, all her major anxieties and stresses have disappeared.

"I still worry at times," she told me, "especially when a big bill comes in or the house payment is due. But even those worries seem less important somehow. In the past, I'd often find it hard to get to sleep because of worrying. That doesn't happen anymore."

A Morning Ritual

This brief ritual will ensure that you start every day feeling positive and upbeat. When you first wake up lie still for about sixty seconds, then tell yourself you're about to start a wonderful day. Think of some of the activities you'll be doing during the day, and see yourself handling them effortlessly and with great enjoyment.

Give thanks to the universal life force for the gift of life and the opportunity to make the most of every day. If you're religious, you might like to say a prayer at this point.

Stretch luxuriously, smile, and tell yourself you're going to make the most of everything that happens to you during the day. Once you've done this, get out of bed and start your day.

Every now and again during the day, remind yourself that this is going to be a wonderful day. You'll find that every aspect of your life will improve as a result of this simple ritual. You'll be more positive, less judgmental, and more patient. You won't get upset or uptight over small delays or mishaps. You'll be more tolerant of others, and find yourself smiling more than ever before. You'll also sleep better as, when you review the day you've just enjoyed, you'll automatically think about the good things that happened. These are rich rewards for a ritual that can be performed in a couple of minutes.

A Purification Ritual

Water has always been associated with purification. Even the simple act of washing your hands and face can be turned into a ritual if you approach it with the thought that the running water will carry away all your stresses and concerns.

Taking a bath or a shower provides an excellent opportunity to deliberately let go of tension, worries, and stress. The ritual starts as you turn on the water and finishes when you've completed drying yourself afterward. I like to start and finish this ritual by taking three slow, deep breaths.

While you're in the shower, imagine the water carrying away all your worries and concerns. Allow the water to relax and soothe every muscle of your body. Say to yourself: "I release all the problems and stresses in my life. I let go of all the negativity, and feel more and more positive as I let all my concerns go down the drain."

If you're taking a bath, imagine the water absorbing all your stresses and concerns. Say to yourself: "I release all the problems and stresses in my life. All the negativity is being released into the water and has lost its power to affect me any longer." When you empty the bath, imagine all of your problems disappearing down the drain, leaving you revitalized, purified, and ready for anything.

A Confidence-Building Ritual

This simple ritual can be done anywhere you happen to be and should be performed anytime you feel the need for confidence, strength, or additional support. All you need do is ask the universal life force for whatever it is you desire.

Inhale, hold your breath for a few seconds, and exhale slowly. Speak, silently or aloud, to the universal life force. You might say something like, "God *(Father, Mother, Universal Spirit, Allah, or whatever name you choose)*, I need your help. In just a few minutes I'm going to need plenty of confidence, as I'm going to ask my boss for a raise *(or whatever it is you need the confidence for)*. I've worked hard and deserve a pay increase *(or whatever it is you need)*, but I need your help to provide me with the necessary confidence to ask for it. Thank you for all your help and support."

Take three slow, deep breaths to symbolically fill you with all the confidence you need, and then do whatever it is you require the additional confidence for.

A Nighttime Ritual

This ritual can be performed in bed before going to sleep. The intention is to let go of any negativity that you may have taken on during the day.

Make yourself as comfortable as you can. Think about all the good things that happened during the day. Enjoy reliving them again. Once you've covered all the positive experiences, make a mental list of all the negative things that occurred during the day. Try to look at them dispassionately. See if you could have handled the situations in a calmer, gentler way.

Think about what you learned from the experiences. After examining each experience, say to yourself: "I'm grateful for the opportunity to learn. I'm sorry for any mistakes I made during the day. I forgive myself for the hurt I caused others, and I forgive others for the hurt they caused me. I let go of all the negativity. I am a calm person, and I can now go to sleep in peace."

Take a slow, deep breath and allow yourself to drift off to sleep. If you make this ritual a part of your everyday life, you'll find your sleep peaceful, restful, and restorative to your body and soul. You'll also wake up in the morning full of energy and looking forward to a good, positive, productive day.

A Journal Ritual

Writing in a journal is a revealing, and frequently healing, exercise. It can be highly therapeutic to record all your problems in a journal, and you'll be able to view them in a completely different way when you read what you've written.

You can record anything you wish in your journal. Naturally, your hopes and dreams should be recorded, as well as your successes and failures. This is an excellent way to free yourself of worries and concerns. Many people use their journals to help them get in touch with the universal life force, as the exercise brings them closer to the divine.

Writing in your journal is a ritualistic act, especially if it is performed in the same place at the same time on a regular basis. Every Sunday evening, a lady I know has a leisurely bath and then creates a circle of candles around her desk before starting to write in her journal. This puts her in the right frame of mind, and her words flow quickly and easily. She is a successful businesswoman with an extremely stressful job. Her intention is to restore her soul and gain peace and serenity.

"Writing in my journal keeps me sane," she told me. "I look forward to Sunday evening all week. Laurence [her husband] knows that I need this quiet time and stays well away until I've finished. As I soak in the bath, I think about the week that has just gone and the things I have to do in the week to come. I don't think about what I'm going to write. Sometimes, I'm amazed at what comes out when I start. I love lighting the candles and spend quite a bit of time placing them in a circle around my desk. I light them in a clockwise order, and put them out in a counterclockwise order.

"There's no particular reason why I do it that way. It must have felt right the first time I did it, so I've continued doing it the same way. When I've finished writing, I read over what I've written, and then I close my journal. I place both hands on the cover and say a brief prayer of thanks. Then I get up, put out the candles, and go downstairs to enjoy a glass of wine with Laurence." Although she didn't mention it, the glass of wine following her ritual could be considered a continuation of the ritual or possibly a separate ritual.

A Walking Ritual

With a little bit of thought, you can turn any walk into a ritual. This particular walking ritual should ideally be done in the countryside. However, if you live in a large city, you might choose to do it in a park. In a public place, such as a park, I suggest you do it early in the morning or toward dusk in the evening, as you don't want too many distractions while you perform your ritual. You don't need to be entirely on your own, though, as no one will have any idea that you're performing a ritual.

Think of something in your life that you'd like to release and choose a small object to symbolize it. As this object will be discarded during the ritual, choose something that's environmentally friendly. You also need to think of a quality that you'd like to have in your life. Again, choose a small object to symbolize this. Choose the entrance to your sacred space. If you're doing this in a public place, perhaps the entrance to the park will also become the entrance to your sacred space.

When it's time to take the walk, walk for as long as you wish. Think about whatever it is you're intending to release. Hold or touch the symbolic object that represents it. When you've walked as far as you intend to go, stop, gaze at the symbolic object in your hand, and thank it for serving a role in your life. Tell it you no longer want or need it and you're letting it go. Thank it one more time, and then toss the symbolic object backward over your shoulder. As you let it go, visualize yourself experiencing a great sense of release and relief as the unwanted quality is left behind forever. As it's now gone from your life, it's important that you don't turn around to see where it landed.

As you walk away, think about the new quality that you're welcoming into your life. You have plenty of room for it, as you've let go of something that had outworn its use. Touch or hold whatever it is you chose to represent your new intention. From now on, whenever you see or touch this object, you'll immediately become aware of the new quality it has brought into your life.

Continue thinking about the new quality for as long as you can. When you find your mind drifting off and thinking about other things, let your thoughts go and continue walking to the entrance, confident that the new intention has embedded itself in your mind and that you'll exhibit whatever the quality is from this day forward.

You can repeat this ritual as often as you wish. However, on future walks you don't need to think about the quality you let go, as it was left behind on your first walk. Instead, think about the new quality you've invited into your life. Hold or touch the symbol you chose to represent it throughout the walk.

Sending Love

This ritual can be performed anywhere. I especially enjoy performing this when I'm out walking, but I've also done it while riding on a bus, driving my car, and sitting quietly at home.

Before starting, you need to clarify your intent. Are you going to send love to a particular person, a group of people, or maybe humanity as a whole? You're not restricted to people, either. You might, for instance, choose to send love to animals and plants. If you're out walking, you might decide to send love to every living thing you pass. A friend of mine in New York sends love to all his fellow passengers whenever he rides the subway.

Once you have your intention clearly in mind, all you have to do is silently send out thoughts of love to whomever it happens to be. When I take my daily walk, I send out love to the people and animals I encounter. I live on the edge of a city, and I walk in the countryside. Consequently, I send love to people, cats, dogs, chickens, goats, sheep, horses, and even alpacas on a daily basis.

Interestingly, although I'm constantly sending out love by doing this, I always return home feeling revitalized and full of love. It seems that the more love you send out, the more you have yourself.

four

Your Spiritual Journey

We're all on a spiritual journey, even though many people try to ignore this. Spiritual people realize there is more to life than simply being born, living for a while, and then dying. These people have their spirituality affirmed in many ways through hunches, feelings, intuitions, and signs. Spiritual people experience just as many difficulties and problems as anyone else, but they try to go with the flow and learn from every experience.

To be spiritual means you recognize the presence of the divine in every area of life. Life is easier when you're in touch with your own spirituality as it means you're contacting your soul—your own true self.

Fortunately, all rituals are spiritual in nature and can make our path through life smoother, richer, and more fulfilling. It's not hard to create your own rituals. As long as you consider whatever it is to be important enough to warrant a ritual, and there is an intention behind it, you can turn almost any action into a ritual. Your thoughts about a particular action or activity are all that are required.

Let's assume you're going to meet a friend at your local coffee shop. If this is something you do on a regular basis, it's already a ritual. If this is a rare or unusual occurrence, think about turning it into a ritual. Your intention might be to enjoy catching up with your friend. However, you could easily increase the importance of the ritual.

Spending time with the special people in your life has the potential to be a spiritual experience, as you nurture your soul whenever you spend quality time with the people you love. In this instance, the sacred space is the coffee shop. If you meet your friend with this in mind, the meeting will be just as much fun as usual, but will gain a whole new spiritual dimension.

Spending time outdoors appreciating the wonders of nature can be highly spiritual. In fact, you don't even need to be outdoors. Many years ago, I was having a meal in a restaurant in Minneapolis in late October and was excited when I looked out the window and saw falling snow. The people I was eating with weren't quite so happy, as it was a sign of an early winter, but I was visiting and was overwhelmed by what was for me an extremely unusual sight.

Spending time with animals or children can be highly spiritual. It's a wonderful experience to see the world through someone else's eyes, and to momentarily experience the divine in all creation.

You can turn almost any activity into a spiritual experience if you approach it in the right state of mind. If you're vacuuming your home, for instance, you can turn this simple task into a ritual with the intent that you're vacuuming with love and are blessing your home.

Spiritual rituals help people find a purpose in life. They enable people to nurture their souls, find their innermost selves, connect with others, and gain a closer connection with the architect of the universe.

Here is a selection of spiritual rituals to consider.

Prayer

Prayers are by far the most common of all spiritual rituals. Saying grace before meals is a spiritual ritual. Many people pray before going to bed at night. You can recite or read a prayer at any time of the day or night.

I love reading the Prayer of St. Francis out loud. I know St. Francis probably didn't write this prayer, but whenever I read it the words have special meaning for me, and I feel myself in the presence of the divine.

If you remain alert to them, you'll find numerous opportunities for prayer every day. I once met a woman who prayed for the sick every time she drove past a hospital. You might see a distressing news report on television and pray for the people involved. You can pray for politicians, doctors, nurses, dentists, teachers, shop assistants, and all the other people you encounter in your life. You can pray for animals, too. You don't need to worry about what you say in your prayers, either. It's the intent that matters.

You can pray for yourself as well. Once you've said your prayer, let it go. Trust that it will be answered, and whatever happens will be for your highest good.

A large percentage of the population prays. According to a Gallup poll, 90 percent of people in the United States pray, and 60 percent of these consider prayer to play an important part in their lives (Poloma and Gallup 1991).

You can communicate with the universal life force whenever you wish. If you approach prayer as a ritual that enables you to communicate with the divine, you'll find it will strengthen your relationship with the architect of the universe (God, Allah, Infinite Spirit, etc.).

Gratitude Ritual

Being grateful for what you have, rather than focusing on what you don't have, enables you to focus on the positive aspects of your life. Gratitude is a spiritual practice, and a regular ritual of writing down all the good things that happen to you on a daily basis will enhance your life enormously.

You can also use your feelings of gratitude to help others. All you need is a small container and a number of coins. Sit quietly and think about all the things you're grateful for. Every time you think of something, place a coin in the container. At the end of this ritual, or when the container is full, donate the money to your favorite charity.

Practicing unconditional gratitude is a highly effective way to develop spiritually. It's easy to be grateful when good things occur. However, it's a different matter when life is proving difficult and painful. Many people moan and groan when bad things occur and fail to learn the spiritual lessons that are present in every experience. Other people, by far the minority, accept these experiences as part of the rich tapestry of life, and use them to grow inwardly. Here's an interesting ritual you can perform when life is not going your way.

1. Sit down comfortably, close your eyes, and take several slow, deep breaths.

2. Think of something good that has happened to you recently. It doesn't need to be anything major. It might be someone letting you change lanes in rush hour traffic. It could be a chance meeting with a good friend. Relive the experience in your mind, and give thanks to the architect of the universe for making it happen.

3. Think of a person or animal you love. Allow yourself to relive the feelings you have when you spend time with this special person or pet. Again give thanks to the architect of the universe for bringing you together.

4. Think of an occasion when you were honored or appreciated by others. This doesn't necessarily mean something huge, such as a presidential citation. It could be your fifth birthday party.

Allow yourself to relive this special event in your mind, and then thank the architect of the universe for enabling it to happen.

5. Think about your present situation and what is going on in your life. Accept that the experience is occurring and there's nothing you can do about it. You can become angry and upset, but you realize there's no point in doing that, as it won't make the situation go away. You can also tell yourself that you've experienced difficult times in the past, and that eventually the problems were resolved and life got back to normal. You know that this problem will soon be behind you, too.

6. In your imagination, thank the architect of the universe for giving you a chance to grow spiritually. Ask how you can turn the experience to your highest good and how you can make the most of your current situation.

7. Sit quietly for a minute or two, paying attention to your breathing, and wait to see what ideas and insights pop into your mind.

8. Finish the ritual by saying thank you to the architect of the universe and affirm that you're growing spiritually.

9. Count from one to five, open your eyes, stretch, and when you feel ready, get up.

You should repeat this ritual as often as necessary until the difficulty has been resolved.

Communing with Nature

Spending time in nature can also be considered a spiritual act. Have you ever been moved by a glorious sunset or a spectacular view? There's a waterfall not far from my home that we visit every now and again. I love walking beside the river while listening to the sounds of the waterfall. It's always a magical moment to turn a corner and see the surging water. Throughout history, there have been many nature-centered religions, and it's easy to understand why, as nature is full of the creations of the architect of the universe.

Many people get so involved in their everyday concerns that they fail to see the incredible beauty of the nature that surrounds them. Try taking a walk with the express intention of noticing as much of nature's beauty as you can. You'll return home revitalized with a new sense of wonder at the perfection of this world we live in.

If you do this, please leave any recorded music at home. Recently I went on a nature walk with about twenty other people. Four of them listened to music as they walked, and they totally missed the wonderful, joyful sounds of nature as well as the peace and tranquility that comes from walking in silence.

Creativity

There's a special joy in creating something that can only be described as spiritual. Artists, musicians, and writers all experience moments when they seem to be a channel for the divine. Anyone who creates something has the potential to make this connection. My son-in-law is a useful man to know, as he enjoys solving computer problems. He almost always appears to go into a trance state while doing this.

Even people who do what might seem like mundane work can do this. Many years ago, I interviewed a street cleaner who worked in the red-light district of the city I live in. He had written two books about his life helping people who were often in desperate straits, and he had become a local celebrity as a result. He told me how he loved cleaning the streets, as he was improving the area, and he did the job to the very best of his ability. I watched him for a while after the interview, and the serene look on his face and the care and attention he paid to his work told me clearly that he was making a spiritual connection.

Next time you're doing a task that you don't normally pay much attention to, do the opposite. Focus on it, and do the very best job that you can. You'll find the experience uplifting and, yes, spiritual.

Singing and Dancing

Singing and dancing are excellent ways to live in the moment and to express your love for the divine. You can do this whenever and wherever you happen to be. Many people sing in the shower, and this is an excellent place to do it, as the water from the shower purifies you as you make an offering of song. It makes no difference if you can sing in tune or not.

The same thing applies with dancing. You can do it inside a locked room, if you don't want anyone to see you. Let yourself go, and make all the moves you might not be brave enough to do in front of an audience.

Every time you sing or dance you're making an offering to the divine.

Postal Ritual

This is a particularly enjoyable ritual to do as it provides pleasure to both you and to someone you love. Several times, after performing this ritual, I've heard back from the other person telling me that my message arrived at the perfect time, as something was going on in their life and they needed to hear something positive.

Ahead of time, decide to whom you'd like to send a loving message. This is likely to be someone you aren't able to see often, but who is a good friend. You might like to make a list of these people and perform this ritual for each of them in turn.

Required: One card or a sheet of good quality paper, a pen, and an envelope.

1. Sit down quietly and think about the person you're going to send the card or letter to. Think about all the qualities you love and admire about this person.

2. Close your eyes and visualize this person as clearly as you can. In your imagination, recall a scene where this person made you laugh or you did something special together.

3. Open your eyes and write a message to this person, saying how much he or she means to you

and how your life has been enriched by their love and friendship.

4. Address the envelope while sending thoughts of love to your friend.

5. Send more love to your friend as you post the envelope. Think what he or she will experience when the envelope is delivered. It's not that common to receive a personal letter in the post nowadays, and your friend will feel your energy and your intention before he or she opens and reads it.

Random Acts of Kindness

Helping other people is an excellent way to enhance your spirituality. Most people are willing to help friends and family, but not everyone is prepared to help complete strangers. When I was a teenager, a secretary in the company I worked for regularly put coins in parking meters to prevent the owners of the cars from getting parking tickets. Fifty years later, I still remember her random acts of kindness, and I'm sure she derived spiritual benefit as a result. You might start by buying a coffee for the person in line behind you at your coffee shop.

You can also practice this without spending money. If you have a large number of groceries and the person behind you has only a few items, you can let him or her move ahead of you. The person will be pleased and surprised, and the feelings of joy and happiness you receive from making the gesture will last throughout the day.

Random acts of kindness are effectively a brief ritual in which you're expressing your humanity by doing something worthwhile for others for no reason at all. These small acts might seem to be almost nothing to you, but they can sometimes mean the world to other people. Many years ago, I read about a man who was intending to commit suicide but changed his mind after receiving a smile from a stranger he passed in the street. Even something as small as a smile can change lives.

Healing

Healing rituals provide benefits to the person being healed and also help the people doing the healing. Every now and again, we all need healing for the spiritual, emotional, mental, and physical aspects of our being. Rituals of this sort also create a close connection with the spiritual world.

You can turn any gemstone into a healing stone. Find a stone that appeals to you, hold it in your cupped hands, and talk to it. Tell it how you wish it to help you send healing energies to a specific person, yourself, a group of people, or humanity as a whole. Wait until you receive some sort of response from the gemstone. This will probably occur as a sense or a feeling that the gemstone has agreed to help.

You can now keep the gemstone in a pocket or purse. If you keep it in a purse, you might like to place it inside a small velvet bag to protect it. Several times a day take out the crystal and hold it in your hands. This energizes it. Think of the person or people you wish to send healing energies to and visualize the gemstone helping you do this.

A Forgiveness Ritual

At Christmastime in 1957, Martin Luther King Jr. (1929–1968) preached a sermon called "Loving Your Enemies." He wrote the sermon while in prison for nonviolent civil disobedience during the Montgomery bus boycott. His sermon began with these words: "We must develop and maintain the capacity to forgive. He who is devoid of the capacity to forgive is devoid of the power to love. … There is some good in the worst of us and some evil in the best of us."

Alexander Pope (1688–1744), the English poet, wrote: "To err is human; to forgive, divine." Although this sounds simple, it's sometimes extremely hard to put into practice.

Forgiveness doesn't mean condoning another person's actions. It doesn't mean you need to forget what the person did, either. Forgiving means that you're letting go of whatever it was and moving forward again.

Here's a simple ritual that will help you forgive someone for whatever he or she did to you.

1. Sit down comfortably, close your eyes, and take several slow, deep breaths. Allow yourself to relax as much as you can.

2. Think of all the reasons why you should forgive this person. These might include improvements to your health, stress levels, self-esteem, and peace of mind.

3. Visualize the moment when this person hurt you. In your mind's eye picture it as if it were on a small black-and-white television set. Tell yourself: "I'm letting go of this now." Visualize the television set becoming smaller and smaller and fainter and fainter until it completely disappears.

4. Pray sincerely for the person you are forgiving. Visualize him or her as clearly as you can, and imagine him or her surrounded by divine light. Ask God *(architect of the universe, Divine Spirit, Allah, etc.)* to protect and look after this person.

5. Ask for forgiveness for any hurts you may have done to others.

6. Say a prayer of thanks in your normal manner.

7. Visualize yourself in the near future on a huge, brightly colored television set. See how happy and contented you are now that you've forgiven the person who hurt you.

8. Take a few slow, deep breaths and open your eyes. Monitor your progress. If you find you're still feeling anger or resentment toward the other person, repeat this ritual until every piece of emotion connected to the incident has vanished.

Spiritual Knots

Tying knots in a length of rope or cord has played a popular role in ritual magic for thousands of years.

Here's an interesting ritual intended to enhance your connection with the universal life force.

Required: A nine-foot length of cord. If you know how to braid, you might start with three lengths of cord and braid them together while thinking of your desire to become closer to the divine.

You'll also need to recite a traditional poem while tying each of the nine knots you're going to tie on the cord:

By knot of one, my ritual's begun.

By knot of two, my hopes come true.

By knot of three, divinity.

By knot of four, I need you more.

By knot of five, I'll live and thrive.

By knot of six, my goal is fixed.

By knot of seven, I reach for heaven.

By knot of eight, I welcome fate.

By knot of nine, I reach for the divine.

The knots need to be tied on the cord in a particular sequence as you say the rhyme. The first knot is tied at the left end of the cord, and the second is tied at the right end. The third knot is tied in the center of the cord. The fourth knot is tied halfway between the center and the left end knots. The fifth knot is tied halfway between the center and the right end knots. At this stage there are five knots on the cord, and they divide the cord into quarters. The sixth knot is tied between the knot at the left end and the knot marking the first quarter. The seventh knot is tied between the knot at the right end and the knot marking the start of the fourth quarter. The eighth knot is tied in the center of the second quarter, and the ninth knot is tied in the middle of the third quarter.

When you've completed this, make a circle out of the cord on the ground and stand inside it. Close your eyes, and say a prayer. Allow yourself to feel the presence of the divine for as long as you wish. Place the cord somewhere safe.

Every day for the next nine days, you'll untie one of the knots. They must be untied in reverse order to the way they were tied initially. Consequently, on the first day you'll untie the last knot to be tied, and on the ninth day you'll untie the first knot to be tied. Each day, as you do this, think of the life force inside you, the blessings you have in your life, and your spiritual connection to the architect of the universe.

On the ninth day, you'll untie the last knot. If you wish, you can repeat the ritual by waiting one day and then tying another nine knots in the same order as before.

God Within Ritual

Namaste is a respectful Hindu greeting that people use when they meet and say good-bye to others. Namaste means "I bow to the divine in you." It is usually accompanied by bowing the head and holding both palms together with the fingers pointing upward and the thumbs close to the heart. It's a wonderful greeting as it acknowledges the divine in everyone. Effectively, one person's soul is recognizing and appreciating the soul of someone else.

Here is a namaste ritual that you can practice for a whole day. From the moment you wake up, look for the divine in everyone you encounter. You don't need to actually bow, make a prayer gesture with your hands, or say "namaste," although you can, if you wish. In your mind's eye, gently bow to everyone you're in contact with during the day and sense their spiritual energy.

This ritual will change the way in which you meet people for the first time. You, like everyone else, make instant decisions about people based on their looks, posture, tone of voice, and facial expressions. It's difficult to change the first impressions you make when meeting someone. However, if you pause long enough to see the divine inside this person, you can start looking for the person's good qualities, rather than the bad.

You'll find this particularly useful when dealing with difficult or challenging people. My relationship with a server at a local store changed immediately once I started doing this. This man is known as Mr. Grumps to virtually all of his customers, as he appears to enjoy being rude and belligerent toward them. Once I deliberately looked for the divine in him, he became more helpful and cooperative, at least to me. I've yet to see him smile, but I'm working on that.

If you try this for a day, you're likely to continue doing it, as you'll see everyone you encounter in a new light, and you will realize that they are, like you, part of God.

Blessing Ritual

This is an interesting ritual that you'll enjoy doing. A large part of the enjoyment comes before the ritual even starts. This is because you have to go for a walk and find four items that you can relate to your life in some way. If, for instance, you find a feather, you might relate that to the fact that birds fly through the air and you need air to breathe. You might consider it a spiritual gift if you relate it to an angel's wing. A nail might relate to practicality if you're a home handyman. It might relate to the fact that you need to find a carpenter to do some repairs in your home. It could relate to a challenge, as you've been putting off a minor carpentry job at home because you're not sure you can do it. An acorn could mean the start of something new. If you've been delaying a project, the acorn might be a sign that it's time to act. It doesn't matter how tenuous the connection may be, as long as you find one.

I tend to look for interesting items and think about connections later. Consequently, I might return home with twelve items, and then decide which four are most relevant to me at the time.

Once you've found the items, place them on your altar, or a table, in front of you. I usually light a white candle and place it in the center of the table behind the four objects.

1. Pick up the first object and think about what it means to you. Is it a gift, such as an angel's wing feather? Is it a talent, such as a nail if you're a carpenter? Is it a challenge, if it's something you're not feeling confident about? If you have a reasonable amount of privacy, talk out loud to the object, telling it how it relates to you, and blessing it for appearing in your life at the perfect time. If you're unable to speak out loud, mentally send your thoughts to the object.

2. Replace the first item on your altar and pick up the second item. Repeat the process and finish by blessing it and thanking it for appearing at the right time.

3. Repeat step two with the remaining two objects.

4. Sit down and gaze at the objects on your altar. Wait and see if any insights or ideas come to you. I don't believe the four objects are selected randomly, and feel they're found and picked up for a spiritual purpose.

On one occasion, at this stage in the ritual, I realized that all four objects related to one goal. It was a powerful message that told me I'd been neglecting something important that I'd been putting off. Usually, the four items relate to completely different areas of life, and usually the message each one brings to the ritual is clear and obvious.

5. When you're ready, say a sincere thank you to each of the objects in turn. Thank God (by whatever name you choose) for sending you valuable information through the objects. Continue by thanking the divine for your powerful mind, healthy body, and immortal soul.

6. Snuff out the candle to mark the end of the ritual. If possible, leave the objects on your altar for an hour or two.

I like to keep the objects I've collected for a day or two, and then redistribute them in the area where I found them. Every now and again, a particular object will resonate so much that I keep it as a lucky charm or amulet.

Mandala Ritual

The word *mandala* comes from a Sanskrit word that means "circle." Mandalas can be of any shape, but are usually circular pictures that show that life is never ending. Interestingly, circular mandalas predate the invention of the wheel, as they have been found in ancient rock engravings (Jaffé 1990). The rose windows found in many cathedrals are good examples of mandalas, as are the halos surrounding holy people in numerous religious paintings. The twelve signs of the zodiac are usually shown in the form of a mandala. Even the ground plan of Washington, DC, is a mandala.

Carl G. Jung (1875–1961), the Swiss psychiatrist and psychotherapist, used mandalas extensively in his psychotherapy work to identify and treat emotional disorders in his patients. He also drew them frequently for himself. Jung wrote: "The mandala is an archetypal image whose occurrence is attested throughout the ages. It signifies the wholeness of self. This circular image represents the wholeness of the psychic ground or, to put it in mythic terms, the divinity incarnate in man" (Jung 1963).

Mandalas are frequently used for meditation purposes. They are often drawn for spiritual purposes, too, and constructing your own mandalas clearly reveals what is going on in your life at the time you drew them.

Traditional mandalas are usually made up of geometrical shapes, such as triangles, circles, and squares, but abstract mandalas can include anything you wish. Fortunately, there is no right or wrong way to construct a mandala, and no artistic ability is necessary. Many people start by drawing a dot, known as a *bindu*, in the center of the circle, and use this as a starting point.

Here's a suggested mandala ritual.

Required: A pad of paper and several colored pens, pencils, or markers. I usually use a dinner plate as a template to draw a circle on the sheet of paper I'll be drawing on. You might like to play some relaxing music during the ritual.

1. Think about your intention. You might want to develop spiritually. You might desire a closer relationship with your partner. You might want to complete a particular project that's been causing you difficulty at work. Focus on your intention for as long as you can.

2. Pick up one of your pens and start drawing anything you wish inside the circle while continuing to think about your intention. You can draw lines, pictures, geometrical shapes, solid blocks of color, or anything else that occurs to you. Change colors every now and again. Don't stop to evaluate or critique what you're doing. Allow your creativity to take over and draw whatever it wishes while you think about your intention and how good you'll feel once it's achieved.

3. Once you've finished, look at your mandala. You'll feel the energy of your intention, and you may even notice other things that your subconscious mind added to make your mandala more effective. You can also interpret the different colors you chose to use:

Red relates to enthusiasm, passion, and energy.
Pink relates to love, femininity, and intuition.
Orange relates to creativity, self-awareness, and cooperation.

Yellow relates to communication, learning, and happiness.

Green relates to healing, love of nature, and hard work.

Blue relates to freedom, variety, and excitement.

Purple relates to spirituality and wisdom.

White relates to purity and spiritual aspiration.

Black relates to secrets, responsibilities, and individuality.

4. Hang up your mandala somewhere where you'll see it frequently. Each time you notice it, it will remind you of your intention.

If you wish, you can repeat this ritual several times, spaced approximately a week apart. Display your mandalas in a row. Every now and again, draw another one, and you'll be able to observe how your mandalas change as you get closer and closer to your goal.

Mandala of Protection

We tend to think we can withstand anything that life throws at us, but in actuality we all experience negativity, tension, and stress, often on a daily basis. Over a period of time, these negative influences weaken us and destroy our feelings of well-being and happiness.

Fortunately, you can eliminate this negativity from your life by drawing a mandala of protection.

Required: a pad of 8.5" x 11" paper and a set of colored pens, pencils, or markers

1. Think of your intention of eliminating negativity and tension from your life.

2. Place the pad of paper on the table in front of you with the long side facing you. This is known as the landscape position. Draw a bindu in the center of the page.

3. Place your hands in a relaxed position on the paper with your thumbs touching each other below the bindu. Notice where your little fingers are placed. Draw a small circle at the places where the tips of your little fingers are resting.

4. Close your eyes, and again think of your intention and what your life will be like once you're free from stress and tension.

5. When you feel ready, open your eyes, pick up a pen or a marker, and start drawing anything that relates to your desire for protection. The only requirement is that whatever you draw includes the two circles where your little fingers rested.

6. Use as few or as many colors as you wish. Stop as soon as you feel you've done enough. I've seen protection mandalas consisting of just a few lines, and others that look like magnificent works of art.

7. Whenever you feel the need for protection or want to eliminate the pressures and stresses of life place your mandala on a table and rest your hands on it with your thumbs touching and the tips of your little fingers resting inside their

circles. This creates a circle of protection that includes your chest, arms, hands, and thumbs. You also gain additional power and protection from a second circle that runs from the thumb of one hand, across the back of your hand to your little finger, across your mandala to your other little finger, and on to the thumb of that hand where it starts the whole circle all over again.

Visualize these two circles of protection and keep your hands in position until you feel calm and in control.

This mandala can also be used to provide energy if you're feeling rundown or overtired.

Connecting with the Source Ritual

Many people go through life with a feeling that they're not fulfilled or that something is missing. This is usually caused by a lack of contact with their innate spirituality. This ritual is intended to help you reconnect, or make a stronger connection, with the Source *(God, or whatever name you choose to use)*.

Required: A comfortable chair and 20 to 30 minutes.

1. Sit down in your comfortable chair, take three slow, deep breaths, and close your eyes.
2. Focus on relaxing your entire body. You can do this by tensing and then relaxing the muscles in

different parts of your body, or you might prefer to start at your feet and gradually relax all of
the muscles in your body until you feel totally
relaxed.

3. When you feel completely relaxed sit quietly
and pay attention to your breathing. Do this for
at least a minute.

4. When you feel ready, start a conversation with
your higher self, the Source inside you, in your
mind. Realize that this Source is the same
Source that's inside everyone. We are all one.
Acknowledge that the Source is always with you,
no matter where you are, or what you're doing.
Allow yourself to listen to your soul.

5. Express your gratitude to your soul for its wisdom and guidance. Make a circle with the
thumbs and first fingers of each hand, and then
gently rub the fingers and thumbs together while
telling yourself that you're fully connected to the
Source. Continue doing this for about a minute.

6. Take a slow, deep breath, hold it for a few seconds, and exhale slowly. Repeat this twice,
and then bring yourself back to full conscious
awareness by slowly counting from one to five.

7. Open your eyes. Do not move until you feel
you're completely back in the present.

8. When you feel ready, get up and have something to eat and drink before carrying on with
your day. If time permits, do something that

nurtures your soul. You might spend time outdoors enjoying the wonders of nature, play with
a child, take a dog for a walk, read a good book,
or do anything else that makes you feel good.

9. Allow at least an hour to pass, and then gently rub your thumbs and first fingers together.
Pause and see what happens. This small, almost
invisible movement should bring you into
immediate contact with the Source. Express
your thanks and carry on with whatever it was
you were doing.

You should repeat this ritual as often as necessary
to obtain an immediate connection with your Source.

Spiritual Breathing Ritual

An ancient mystical concept says that breath is a gift
from the divine, and must be returned when the individual dies. It's interesting to reflect that the very first
thing you did when you were born was breathe, and
the very last thing you'll do will be your final breath.
Blowing out the candles on your birthday cake provides proof that your life is continuing beyond the
years indicated by the candles on your cake. In this
case, breath is a symbol of life.

There's a strong link between breath and spirit
in many religious traditions. God breathed life into
Adam's nostrils and "he became a living soul" (Gene-
sis 2:7). Controlled breathing plays an important role
in the meditation practices of many traditions.

You can practice mindfulness by pausing every so often throughout the day and becoming aware of your breathing. Take slow, deep breaths and temporarily forget everything else. Listen for anything your body may be telling you.

This is a simple ritual that can be done anytime you wish. Say:

1. As I breathe in, I'm calm and relaxed. Breathing out, calm and relaxed.

2. As I breathe in, I'm filled with joy. Breathing out, joy, joy, joy.

3. As I breathe in, I'm filled with love. Breathing out, love, love, love.

4. As I breathe in, I feel fulfilled. Breathing out, fulfilled, fulfilled.

5. As I breathe in, I feel compassion. Breathing out, compassion, compassion.

6. I feel God's presence in every breath. I feel God's presence in every breath.

7. I'm a spiritual being with much to learn. I'm a spiritual being with much to learn.

8. Please help me find my way to you, to you.

You can do this ritual in less than a minute, whenever you feel the need for it. I prefer to do it with my eyes closed, but that's a personal choice and isn't necessary.

Three Breaths Ritual

This short ritual can be done in a matter of seconds, yet it has the power to change your life. All you need to do is pause in whatever you happen to be doing and take three slow, deep breaths. Think a positive thought with each breath. You might, for instance, say to yourself, "I'm a good, valuable, worthwhile human being" on the first breath. You could say, "I send love to everyone I meet" on the second breath, and "I smile with each breath as I gain peace of mind and limitless energy."

If you can, close your eyes while performing this ritual. You can perform it several times a day, if you wish. You'll be amazed at the effect that three deliberate breaths accompanied by positive thoughts will have on your life.

Brahmari Ritual

This is a yogic exercise that uses breath to enhance your spirituality. This ritual is sometimes called "humming bee breath."

1. Sit down in a chair with a straight back. Close your eyes and breathe in through your nose. (Your mouth remains closed for the entire ritual.)

2. Exhale through your nose. As you do this, start humming. Vary the pitch of your hum until you find one that appeals to you.

3. Once you have completely exhaled, breathe in again and start humming as you exhale. Repeat five to ten times.

You'll find that, even if you felt stressed at the start of the ritual, by the end of it you'll feel totally relaxed, calm, and free of stress.

Loving Kindness Ritual

According to legend, the first person to teach loving kindness was Buddha. Apparently, one evening he and a group of followers were meditating in a forest. His followers were frightened by tree spirits, and Buddha taught them loving kindness to eliminate their fears.

Loving kindness involves repeating phrases that send loving thoughts to ourselves, the people we love, acquaintances, people we find hard to get along with, and humanity in general. The idea behind this is that once we have successfully sent loving thoughts to ourselves, we can then see and appreciate the special qualities that everyone possesses, and consequently we send loving thoughts to them, too.

If you perform this ritual regularly, you'll find you'll be able to handle all the challenges that life throws at you with much less stress or tension.

To perform a loving kindness ritual, sit down comfortably, close your eyes, and relax.

1. When you feel ready, visualize yourself. See, or at least sense, yourself sitting down comfortably with your eyes closed.

2. Silently say the following phrases to yourself. Pause for a few seconds after saying each one. You don't need to be word perfect, but ideally you should say each one several times.

   Please fill me with love and compassion.

   Please surround me with protection from harm.

   Please help me to love and be loved in return.

   Please help me to be joyful and contented.

   Please help me enjoy good health.

   Please help me accept and welcome life as it is.

3. Create another phrase or sentence that relates to you as you are now. This could relate to a quality you're trying to develop, but it could just as easily be something that simply pops into your mind while you're performing this ritual.

4. Think of someone you care for and send a loving thought to him or her. You might use one of the thoughts in step 2, such as "Please fill him/her with love and compassion." Alternatively, you can create a new phrase or sentence to send to this person.

5. Think of an acquaintance and send love to him or her. This might be a neighbor, your local FedEx deliveryman, the barista at your local café, or anyone else you interact with but don't really know.

6. Focus on someone who causes aggravation and problems in your life and send love to him or her. Many people, myself included, have had problems with this step. As soon as you think of this person, you're likely to feel angry and aggrieved. Take slow, deep breaths, and tell yourself that you're not your thoughts. It's normal to feel this way, but you're sending love and compassion to him or her anyway. You're likely to feel a deep sense of release and peace once you've done this.

7. Send love and compassion to all humanity. Think of the huge numbers of lonely, unhappy people there are in the world. Think of the homeless people and people who lack clean water to drink. Think of the suffering that so many people endure and send love to all of them.

8. Hold your feelings of love and compassion for as long as you can, and then focus on your breathing. Count slowly from one to five and open your eyes.

Contemplation Ritual

Contemplation is not the same as thinking. The dictionary definition of contemplation is "thoughtful observation." Contemplation allows you to go much deeper than thought and allows you to access information from your heart. In fact, contemplation is sometimes referred to as *prayer of the heart*, as it enables you to learn information that is meaningful and relevant to you.

Contemplation rituals provide valuable insights into what is going on in your life. Contemplation provides many additional benefits, such as enabling you to quieten your mind and remain calm in stressful situations. This enhances your concentration and creativity, improves focus, and helps you become more loving and compassionate.

If you have an altar, you should perform this contemplation ritual in front of it.

Required: a paragraph or two of a sacred text, a pen, and paper. The best spiritual texts to read are ones you find to be inspirational. If you come from a Christian tradition, you might choose a reading from Psalms or the Book of Proverbs. The Bhagavhad Gita, Tao Te Ching, *Confessions of St. Augustine*, *The Tibetan Book of Living and Dying* by Sogyal Rinpoche, *The Imitation of Christ* by Thomas à Kempis, *The Seven Storey Mountain* by Thomas Merton, and *The Varieties of Religious Experience* by William James are all possibilities, but there are thousands of other works you can choose from. The best way to choose a text is to use your intuition.

1. Sit down comfortably and read the passage of text you chose.
2. Close your eyes and focus on your breathing. Notice how your body relaxes as you do this.

3. When you feel relaxed, open your eyes and read the text again. Allow yourself to experience the words at a much deeper level than before.

4. Pick up the pen and write down a few words that relate to what you've just read. You may prefer to draw a simple picture instead of writing a sentence or two.

5. Close your eyes again, and focus on your breathing. After about sixty seconds ask yourself what relevance the passage you've just read has to you and your life.

6. Once you've received an answer to your question, open your eyes and write down anything that came to you about the passage and its relevance to you.

Repeat this ritual once a day for seven days. Continue using the same text, as long as you're continuing to receive fresh insights. Change the text once you've gained everything you can from it.

Pilgrimage Ritual

I regularly talk with people who intend taking a pilgrimage to a sacred place "one day." When I ask them why they haven't done it yet, I receive a variety of answers, usually involving time and money. Of course, if you want to walk the Way of St. James over the Pyrenees Mountains to the Cathedral of Santiago de Compostela in Spain, you'll need to set aside time and money to do this. Fortunately, you can make powerful pilgrimages without traveling far from your home.

A pilgrimage is a journey with the intention of experiencing the sacred. In essence a pilgrimage is an inner journey. You can do this in your hometown. All you need is one day.

Plan ahead. Set the date, and decide where you'll go. Your intention will be to experience the divine.

You might decide to visit a nearby park. There could be a monastery, temple, monument, or other holy place that you could visit. You might choose to enjoy a leisurely walk in the countryside. Decide on your ultimate destination. It might be a small country church or a grove of trees. It could be a scenic spot.

Recently, I made a pilgrimage to a bluff overlooking a beach that is popular with surfers. The last time I'd been there I'd seen a small cairn of stones that someone had made, and I was curious to see if it was still there. I was pleased to discover that it was still there, and that it had grown much larger than the first time I'd seen it. It felt very special to be able to add a stone to it.

You'll also need to decide where you'll eat your lunch, and how you'll return home once you've completed your pilgrimage.

On the day you've decided, prepare a packed lunch and set off on your pilgrimage. Although pilgrimages are associated with walking, it doesn't matter if you need to drive to your starting point. Once you're walking, contemplate everything you do, from your breathing to each individual step you take. Tell yourself you're in the presence of the divine, and imagine a divine presence with you on every step of the way. You'll gradually discover that you won't need to imagine the presence of the divine, as it is with you on every step of the way.

Pause to look at anything that interests you on the route, and see the imprint of the divine in everything you see. Gently dismiss any everyday concerns that come into your mind. Tell these thoughts that you're on a pilgrimage and will worry about them tomorrow.

When you reach your destination, thank the divine for accompanying you on your journey of discovery. You might like to pray, meditate, or simply relax for a while before returning home.

You're likely to feel a sense of excitement and accomplishment after completing your pilgrimage, and these feelings are likely to last for a few days.

The next—and harder—step is to turn every day into a pilgrimage of sorts and to feel the presence of the divine in everything you do every day.

Love

Love may well be the most powerful force in the universe. It's certainly the most important. The saying "Love makes the world go 'round" contains a great deal of truth. Love consists of physical, emotional, and spiritual energy, and falling in love is when most people make contact with their innate spirituality for the first time.

When I mention rituals to people, a large proportion want to know how they can create rituals for love. This is a huge subject. Almost everyone I've spoken to about this subject wanted specific rituals to attract a lover, improve a relationship, end a love affair, stop thinking about a previous relationship, save a marriage, arouse passion, encourage a partner to return, and much more. In many cases, it seemed these people wanted a magic spell that would resolve all of their relationship problems.

With any ritual you do, it's important that it's positive for everyone concerned. It's not a good idea to perform a ritual to make a certain person become attracted to you. Although this might work, it won't end happily if it's something the other person would not agree to.

Loving Yourself Ritual

Before you can love anyone else, you must love yourself. Here's an interesting eye-gazing ritual that you can perform in the bathroom, as all you need is a mirror. You need to gaze into your eyes for the entire ritual.

1. Gaze into your eyes in the mirror. Use a soft, gentle gaze, as this ritual is all about loving yourself. Pay attention to any negative thoughts that come into your mind. Each time you think anything negative, let it go by telling the thought that it's no longer needed and say good-bye to it.

2. After a couple of minutes, you'll notice whether or not your self-talk is predominantly negative

or positive. Some dismissed thoughts may reoccur. When that happens, tell them that you've already dismissed them, and they have no power to affect you ever again.

3. Despite dismissing negative thoughts, you may find yourself experiencing different emotions from time to time. You might feel joy, but you could also experience deep sadness. You might want to laugh, and in the next second experience deep calmness. Long forgotten memories may resurface, and you can relive or discard them. You may even see other people's faces in the mirror.

3. After a few minutes, you may find that your surroundings will tend to fade away and all you'll be aware of is your eyes. You'll also gradually become aware that you can keep or discard any thoughts at all. They are yours, and what you do with them is entirely up to you.

4. You'll gradually realize that despite your ever-chattering mind, your thoughts are not you, as you are perfect. Yes, perfect. Take several slow, deep breaths, and see yourself as the beautiful human being that you are.

5. Gaze at yourself with total acceptance. Tell yourself that you love yourself unconditionally.

6. Continue gazing into your eyes and expressing your love for yourself. You may simply think, *I love you, (name)* over and over again. You might find yourself entering a relaxed, meditative state

where all you need do is think the word *love* every now and again. You might continue silently talking to yourself about accepting yourself as you are, that you are a worthwhile, loving person, and that you are pure love. If your attention drifts, gently bring it back by thinking how much you love yourself.

7. After about ten minutes, smile at your reflection in the mirror. Take a few slow, deep breaths, affirm that you love yourself, and break eye contact.

8. Many people feel light-headed after performing this ritual. Make sure you eat and drink something before starting anything else. You might like to stand barefoot on grass or earth for a few minutes to help become grounded again before continuing on with your everyday activities.

There are various ways in which you can perform this ritual. It can be highly effective to do this in a darkened room with a single candle that provides just enough light for you to gaze into your eyes. You can gaze into the eyes of a partner whom you trust implicitly. You can also do it with nature. You can gaze at a flower or an insect and see what comes into your mind.

Attracting a Partner Ritual

This ritual was taught to me by a dear friend who has been happily married for many years. She told me that she found her husband after performing this rite every evening for two months.

Required: A container of table salt.

1. Sit at a table with the container of table salt in front of you.

2. Close your eyes, take three slow, deep breaths, and think about your desire for the right partner. If you can, visualize the type of person you'd like in your life. Do not think of a specific person.

3. Open your eyes and pour some salt onto the table. Smooth it out, and then draw a stick man and a stick woman in the salt. You don't need any artistic ability for this. The figures should be childlike and look like cartoon figures.

4. Gaze at your picture for five minutes. Imagine different scenes of activities you and this partner would do together. Allow yourself to feel happy and totally fulfilled once this person comes into your life.

5. Imagine you and your salt drawing encircled by a pure white light that fills you with love and protection. Hold this image in your mind for as long as you can.

6. When the image fades, visualize yourself as a powerful magnet that attracts anything it sets its mind on.

7. Gather up the salt on the table into a small pile. Go outside and take a brief walk, sprinkling the salt as you go.

8. Return home certain that you've sent your intention out into the universe and that it will be fulfilled.

Repeat this ritual as often as necessary until the right person appears.

Attraction Ritual Two

This ritual is completely different from the first one, and it takes time to complete.

1. Spring-clean your home and remove from view anything that relates to previous unhappy relationships. Create space in your home for the person you're going to attract. You might set a place at the dinner table or create space in the closet for this person to store his or her clothes.

2. Write down all the qualities you want your next partner to possess and read the list at least once a day. Make any changes or additions as they occur to you.

3. Let go of all your previous relationships. You might do this by writing letters to any people whom you had a serious relationship with. Seal the letters in envelopes and burn them during the course of a ritual. As each one burns away, say thank you to the person concerned. At one

time, he or she played an important role in your life. Consequently, although your letters might be angry or bitter, think only of the positive times you spent together while you're destroying them.

You might prefer to write one letter addressed to all your past relationships, thanking them for playing their part in making you the person you are today. Once you've written it, burn it, tear it up into tiny pieces, or bury it somewhere no one will find it.

4. Do something different or new, ideally something that will help you meet new people. Keep looking for opportunities to meet people and participate in as many as you can.

5. Every night, before you fall asleep, tell yourself that you are a worthwhile person with a great deal to offer in a relationship. Follow this by thinking of the type of person you want to attract, and imagine what your life will be like once he or she appears.

6. Remain positively expectant and confident that the right person is out there looking for you, and that the two of you will meet when the time is right.

Attraction Ritual Three

Before performing this ritual, you will need to collect a number of objects that symbolize love and romance to you. These can be anything at all, as long as they remind you of love when you see them. You might have a dozen completely different symbolic objects, or you might have twelve that all depict the same desire. When I was in Japan many years ago, I met a woman who had a large collection of ceramic butterflies displayed on a wall. She had two of everything. When I asked her about this, she told me that a single butterfly depicted femininity but two butterflies symbolized a happy marriage. She started her collection well before she met her husband, and she credits their meeting to her beautiful butterflies.

You can perform this ritual with as little as one symbolic object. However, somewhere between twelve and twenty would be ideal.

1. Place a comfortable chair in the middle of your room and surround it with a circle of your symbolic objects.

2. Sit down in the chair, make yourself comfortable, close your eyes, and ask the universe to help you achieve your goal of attracting the right person to you. Be as specific as you can. Choose a suitable age group for this person as well as any other attributes or qualities you desire. If you come from a Christian tradition, you might say a prayer at this stage.

3. Open your eyes and look at the object immediately in front of you. Think of your purpose in obtaining this object and the goal this object, and your other objects, is intended to produce.

4. Pause, and see what comes into your mind as you look at this object. If you wish, you can talk to the object, as you're likely to gain additional insights by doing this.

5. Look at the object that is to the right of the first one and repeat steps two and three as you gaze at it.

6. Continue doing this with each object in turn. Move your chair when necessary to make sure you can look at all the objects that are surrounding you.

7. Once you've completed your tour of the circle, close your eyes again and visualize what your life will be like once you've achieved your goal. In your imagination, "see" you and the partner you've attracted in a variety of different situations.

8. Open your eyes and spend as long as you wish inside the circle, happy in the knowledge that you've sent your desire out into the universe.

9. When you're ready, leave the circle. Allow the objects to stay in position for thirty to sixty minutes after you've left the circle, to enable them to continue sending your intention out into the world.

10. Carry one of the objects with you in a pocket or a handbag. Every time you see or touch it, it will remind you of your goal, and you'll start thinking of it again. When you think positive

thoughts about love, you effectively become a magnet that will attract your desire to you.

Happy Marriage Ritual

This ritual is to thank the universe for providing you with a long-lasting, happy relationship. You can perform it in a matter of moments whenever you wish. Let's assume the two of you are enjoying a meal out in a restaurant you haven't been to before.

During a pause in the conversation, gaze at your partner and ask him or her: "Do you know what I'm grateful for?" When your partner responds, continue with something along the lines of: "I'm grateful to you for seeing the best in me, even on bad days. I'm grateful for the love we share, for our beautiful family, and for the fact that we're still together after everything we've been through. I love you. Thanks for being in my life."

Hopefully, your partner will express his or her gratitude too, and you can continue talking about the good things about your relationship. As you're talking, reach across the table and hold his or her hand. You can repeat a simple ritual of this sort whenever you wish. The best time to do it is when the two of you are doing something new or different together.

Window Dressing

We used salt in the ritual to attract a partner. Salt has been used in rituals for thousands of years, mainly for purification and protective purposes. As rituals can be performed using nothing but the power of your mind, some people call anything else that's used in the process "window dressing." However, even these people have to admit that window dressing can increase the drama, power, and effectiveness of any ritual. There is a whole branch of magic known as ceremonial or ritual magic that makes extensive use of window dressing.

If you wish, you can add window dressing to your private rituals. You might, for instance, light a candle before praying. You might play meditation music or display a figurine of a particular god or goddess. You could add herbs, essential oils, and crystals. You might create a special ritual space to work within. All of these things help add importance to your ritual, and gathering them together can be considered a ritual in itself.

Here's an example of a ritual that could be performed without any props, but becomes much more powerful with the addition of candles, coins, and salt.

Prosperity Ritual

Required: An altar, a green or gold altar cloth, two green candles, several coins, and anything that symbolizes wealth and prosperity. (Malachite or green jade are good examples, as they're green, which reminds people of money. Anything green, gold, or round can also be used to symbolize prosperity.)

The altar is any table or flat surface you decide to perform your rituals on. In most rituals, this can be a temporary surface. However, this particular altar needs to be set up for a period of time.

1. Set up the altar. Place a candle on each side of your altar. Place the pile of coins, and any other objects you're using to symbolize prosperity, between them in the center of your altar. Sprinkle a small quantity of salt around and on the altar.

2. Stand in front of your altar. Think about your need for more wealth and prosperity in your life. Light the candle on the left-hand side, followed by the candle on the right. Pick up some of the coins and jingle them in your cupped hands for several seconds. Allow them to slip from your hands one at a time back onto the altar.

3. Say something along the lines of: "Infinite Spirit, I need more money in my life. I especially need it as *(name the main reason, followed by any other reasons you may have)*. I'm prepared to do whatever it takes to receive this amount of money. Please help me with this request. Thank you."

4. Leave the candles burning for as long as you remain in the room. Every time you look in their direction tell yourself that they're attracting money to you. Snuff out the candles when you leave the room.

5. During the next twenty-four hours give a dollar or two to someone who needs it. This symbolically demonstrates your feelings of abundance, as you're so wealthy you can afford to

give money away. As you give, so shall you receive. Believe with every fiber of your being that your generosity will be rewarded.

6. Every day, you need to make an offering on your altar. Light the two candles first. Your offerings can be small gifts of fruit, flowers, herbs, gemstones, or anything else that symbolizes prosperity. You might, for instance, place an orange (round and orange in color) on your altar on the first day, and a small bunch of yellow or golden flowers the next. The offerings need to remain on the altar for twenty-four hours before being replaced.

7. After making your offering, repeat your request, and leave the candles burning for as long as you remain in the room. Continue giving away a dollar or two every day. You'll find that by doing this, you'll gradually develop a prosperity consciousness, and opportunities to make money will come your way.

8. Continue doing this every day for as long as necessary.

Group Candle Ritual

Required: One large white candle and enough smaller candles for everyone participating to hold.

The best time to perform this ritual is at dusk when darkness is gathering. However, this can be created with blinds and curtains. One person is designated the leader. He or she lights the candle and guides the proceedings.

As everyone will speak at some stage during the ritual, this person also indicates when it's time for each person to make a comment.

1. The group sits in a circle around a candle. When the candle is lit, everyone gazes at the flame for a minute or two.

2. The leader asks someone to tell the group what the images created by the flame are indicating to him or her.

3. When the first person has finished speaking, the leader asks someone else to say what he or she is seeing or experiencing.

4. This is continued until everyone has had a turn. One person may have talked about how tiny the flame is compared to the darkness all around. Someone else might refer to the fragility of the flame and how easily it could be blown out. The next person might carry on from that and say that although the flame is fragile, it has the potential to destroy.

5. Once everyone has spoken, the leader recaps what each person said and then makes his or her own comments.

6. The leader then talks about the candle as a symbol of spiritual illumination and how it can also depict a lone human soul. He or she explains how the candle has been a symbol of light and faith for thousands of years and then asks if

anyone in the group has experienced anything of a spiritual nature while gazing at the candle.

7. The leader encourages people to speak. Once they have had their say, the group sits in silence for two or three minutes.

8. The leader asks everyone in the group to blow out the candle. The group sits silent in the darkness for another two or three minutes.

9. The leader lights the central candle again and passes out candles to everyone in the group. They all light their own candle from the central one, and sit down again.

10. The leader again encourages people to share their feelings about the ritual they've just experienced, and then he or she announces that the rite is ended.

Afterward, the participants can have something to eat and drink together. Further insights might come into people's minds at this stage. After conversing for as long as they wish, the participants go their separate ways.

Scripts

The rituals we've looked at so far do not require a prepared script. However, for most group rituals, or for something that you consider to be extremely important, you should at the very least make some notes to ensure that you include everything you want. Here's an example:

Soon-to-be-Born Baby Ritual

This is a brief ritual that I wrote for two friends to welcome a soon-to-be-born baby into the family.

Preparation: Before the guests arrive, fill a basket with small objects, such as crystals, coins, dice, and small toys. Place this at the front doorstep. As the guests arrive, ask them to select one item from the basket. The chosen objects will be presented to the unborn child as lucky charms and protective amulets.

1. When it's time for the ritual to begin, the guests form a circle around a wooden box that will be used to hold the selected objects.
2. The father-to-be steps into the circle and welcomes everyone to the happy occasion.
3. The father-to-be introduces his partner, who joins him in the center of the circle. They kiss and hold hands as she tells family and friends what the upcoming birth means to both of them and how their lives will be enriched in so many ways. When she's finished, the couple embraces.
4. One at a time, the people in the circle bring their symbolic gift and place it into the wooden box.
5. The ritual concludes with the couple saying, "We love and bless you all."
6. Their family and friends respond by saying, "We love and bless you and your new baby."

After the ritual: It's important for all the guests to stay for a while, and eat and drink something with the parents-to-be before leaving. (In actuality, the party went on until the small hours of the next morning. The older guests left early, but most guests were young couples who were happy to stay and celebrate the soon-to-arrive new addition to the hosts' family.)

Now that we've looked at a variety of different rituals, it's time to start learning how to introduce magic into the equation and how to create your own magical rituals.

five

The Power of Magic

The dictionary definition of magic is: "the ability to create a desired result using supernatural agencies or the forces of nature." Here is another definition: "Magic involves the use of supernatural power to influence future events." A personal trainer I know tells his clients to relax quietly, visualize a specific goal, create energy, and direct that energy toward the goal. He knows nothing about magic, but his advice could well be a definition of magic.

My favorite definition comes from Aleister Crowley (1875–1947), the famed British magician and occultist, who defined magic as "the Science and Art of causing change to occur in conformity with Will" (Crowley 1929). Another definition I've always liked is by Florence Farr, one of the leading members of the Hermetic Order of the Golden Dawn. She wrote: "Magic consists of removing the limitations from what we think are the earthly and spiritual laws that bind or compel us. We can be anything because we are All" (Farr 1995). Magic could be described as the ability to make things happen in the way you would like them to.

If you examine the rituals in the previous chapters with these definitions in mind, you'll find that they all have an intention, or purpose, behind them. The purification ritual, for instance, is a method of releasing stress and tension. The confidence-building ritual provides the person with positivity, strength, and confidence. This could be considered magic, as someone lacking in confidence can achieve it as a result of performing a ritual. The future event (confidence) came about "in conformity with Will."

Consequently, magic is an extremely powerful tool that many people use without even knowing they're doing it. If someone sets a goal, for instance, and then achieves it, he or she used the power of intention to create the necessary changes in the universe that enabled the goal to materialize. This person may not call it "magic," but what he or she has done is exactly what a magician would do.

Goal-setters often formalize the desired result by writing it down, or they may simply visualize the desired outcome strongly in their minds. No matter what process they use, they are performing magic. As we all set goals, even something as simple as organizing a dinner party, we're all magicians. Some people are naturally good at it, while others need to work hard to develop their skills. However, magic is a skill anyone can learn.

It might seem hard to believe, but your directed thoughts contain enough power to affect your physical reality. This means you can create the kind of life you want to live. Are you seeking a loving, mutually supporting relationship? Would you like a career that offers more opportunities than your current job? Do you have psychological wounds from the past that you'd like to eliminate? Is there a hobby or skill that you'd like to learn? You can use the power of ritual magic to help you achieve all of these, and much, much more.

Business people frequently talk about the power of intention. This means they're using their thoughts to effect change, and that, as we know, is a definition of magic. Dr. Marilyn Schlitz, president and CEO of the Institute of Noetic Sciences, wrote that intention was "the projection of awareness, with purpose and efficacy, toward some object or outcome" (Schlitz 1995). This is exactly what people do when performing a magic ritual.

Using random-event generators (REG), scientists have demonstrated that the power of thought can influence a particular outcome. In 1979, Dr. Robert Jahn founded the Princeton Engineering Anomalies Research (PEAR) laboratory in the basement of the Engineering School at Princeton University. In this laboratory, Dr. Jahn and Brenda Dunne performed more than 2.5 million trials of an experiment that produced random positive and negative pulses. They demonstrated that participants could influence the REG to produce more positive pulses than negative pulses, or vice versa (Jahn et al. 1987). Naturally, a claim such as this had to be carefully examined, and their results were later replicated by 68 other researchers (Radin and Nelson 1989).

Dr. William Braud of the Institute of Transpersonal Psychology in Palo Alto, California, conducted a lengthy series of experiments that demonstrated the power of human thought on animals, such as fish and gerbils, as well as people. One of his experiments demonstrated how the thoughts of one person could influence the fight-or-flight mechanism of someone else (Schlitz and Braud 1997).

A friend of mine enjoys gambling and always performs a brief ritual before rolling dice. He was extremely interested when I told him that some 73 studies had been conducted that examined the attempts made by 2,500 people to influence the throw of dice. After more than 2.5 million throws, the results clearly demonstrated that thought could influence the outcome. The odds of these results occurring by chance were 10 to the power of 76 to one (Radin 2006).

Performing magic in the form of a ritual forces us to focus on our thoughts, and this strengthens both the magic and the ritual. This is the power of ritual magic.

Psionic Magic

A friend of mine performs what is known as psionic magic. Someone who practices psionics is able to perform paranormal phenomena using nothing but the power of his or her mind. Examples include telepathy, clairvoyance, and psychokinesis. My friend claims that he can perform any magical act psionically. In other words, he needs no sacred space, no magical tools, and no rituals to help him perform magic.

Obviously, there are many advantages to performing magic psionically. My friend can perform his magic instantly, whenever he wishes, as no preparation is necessary. He can perform magic while sitting at his desk at work. He can perform magic while sitting on an airplane flying at thirty thousand feet. He can even perform magic sitting in his car waiting for traffic lights to change.

As it's possible to perform good magic psionically, why would anyone choose to perform ritual magic? My friend and I have discussed this topic on many occasions, and even he reluctantly agreed that a good ritual helps the magician remain clearly focused on the desired outcome. He admitted that as a result of our discussions he usually writes a sentence or two relating to whatever his goal happens to be. He says these words before performing his magic. Even saying one sentence effectively changes what he does from psionic magic to ritual magic.

He also agreed that you must have faith in your ability to perform magic for it to be effective. Again, a good ritual is helpful in this regard. A ritual magician performs a sequence of procedures that are intended to produce the desired result. It's easy to believe, or at least temporarily suspend disbelief, in magic while performing a ritual, especially if the magician has conducted successful ritual magic in the past. It can be hard to generate the same amount of belief while performing psionic magic, which is all done inside your head.

It's also extremely rare for someone to create effective magic using solely the power of the mind. My friend is a highly skilled magician who has been performing magic for more than forty years. It took years of practice and experimentation before he was able to perform psionic magic successfully.

Fortunately, this is not the case with ritual magic, and you will start seeing results right away. Naturally, your skills will develop over time, but there's no reason why you shouldn't experience good results the very first time you perform ritual magic.

Keep Silent

Most people want to tell their family and friends about their successes, but you shouldn't do this with magic. One of the cardinal rules of magic is "keep silent." This is because magic is more effective when it's performed in secret. Even in the twenty-first century, many people have strange ideas about magic and may not approve of your interest in the subject. One of the most terrifying experiences of my life was being chased by a group of born-again Christians who didn't approve of my involvement in magic and intended using violence to discourage me.

Obviously, you can discuss magic with people who are involved in the subject. Exchanging information is one of the best ways to learn and develop your skills.

The Threefold Law

Some people are afraid of magic as they relate it to hexes and curses. Magic is sometimes divided into two categories: white and black magic. White magic is said to be good magic, and black magic is considered evil. In reality, it is magicians who are good or evil. If you are a kind and loving person, you'd never perform a ritual intended to harm someone. A white magician would never knowingly hurt anyone. In practice, I've found it hard to explain white and black magic to people who are afraid of the subject. It's easier to "keep silent."

Another reason to avoid so-called black magic is the magical belief that whatever you put out will be returned to you threefold. If you send out positive wishes to the universe, three times that amount will return to you. Likewise, if you send out bad wishes, in the form of a hex or curse, three times that amount will also come back to you. In other words, you reap what you sow.

Now that we've got this out of the way, we can start working on ritual magic.

six

Ritualistic Tools

There are a number of tools that are traditionally used in ritual magic. You can perform successful rituals without them, but the symbolism provided by these tools gives additional power to the ritual. An athame, or knife, for instance, can be used to symbolically cut away something that is not desired.

I've heard these tools described as "window dressing." This means they possess no power, but they make the ritual look more impressive. I can understand this point of view. If you consider these tools to be nothing more than theatrical props, that's what they'll be. However, if you're willing to use your imagination and believe, at least temporarily, that these "props" are playing an important role in the ritual, they'll increase the effectiveness of your magic.

Different traditions have different requirements. Some have an extensive list of magical tools, while others have only a few. Some insist that you make your own magical tools. Others want you to receive these items as a gift or barter for them. Some traditions are opposed to buying your own magical tools, while others don't care how you obtained them. If you're buying your tools, you should never bargain in an attempt to reduce the price, as this symbolically lowers their value to you. If you think the price is too high, keep searching until you find something suitable in your price range.

Here are the main tools that are used in ritual magic:

Athame

An athame (pronounced a-THAH-may or ATH-a-may) is a double-edged knife. The athame is usually personalized with symbols or words (often written in a secret alphabet). These are written or engraved on the handle or etched on the blade. Forty years ago, I was taught that an athame used for ritualistic purposes had to have a black handle. Knives used to cut herbs or other items that were used in the ritual had white handles.

However, in recent years I've seen people using athames with a large variety of different-colored handles. The color of the handle makes no difference, as long as the knife feels right for you. An athame is used symbolically, and it is never used for cutting any physical object.

A ritual knife can be used in a number of different ways. Knives are cutting instruments. In a ritual, knives are used symbolically as a pointing instrument. They are also used to remove harm and to provide protection. Knives provide focus by concentrating the magical energies into a sharp, straight line. They can also be used to cast the sacred circle.

Some people prefer to use a sword rather than a knife. A sword is used in exactly the same way, but it creates a more dramatic effect, which can be helpful in certain circumstances.

The athame usually symbolizes the air element. However, some traditions associate it with fire.

Wand

Traditionally, wands were made from tree branches, but nowadays they can be made from a variety of different materials, including metals such as pewter, silver, and copper. Usually, these wands have a crystal attached to the top. I use a wooden wand, but that's a purely personal preference, and you should choose a wand that feels right for you. Some magicians have a number of wands that they use for different purposes. They might, for instance, have an apple wand for love magic and an oak wand for fire magic. (The reasons for this will be explained later.)

Wands direct magical energy, and they are commonly used to attract and repel energy and to cast the magic circle. They're also used to evoke the god and the goddess.

In the same way that some magicians prefer a sword to a knife, some people prefer to use a staff, which is effectively a large wand, instead of a wand.

The wand usually symbolizes the fire element. However, some traditions associate it with air.

Chalice

A chalice, or cup, is arguably the most sacred of all tools, and it can be found in almost all religions. The Holy Grail that is featured in the legends about King Arthur is a chalice. The chalice is used to hold liquids, such as water and wine, that are consecrated and used in the ritual. Sharing a cup with others shows how much you trust and honor them.

The chalice is a drinking goblet, which is a cup on a stem, similar to a wine glass. It is usually made of silver, pewter, horn, or earthenware (pottery or ceramic). It should not be made of brass or copper, as these create poison when placed in contact with wine or fruit juice.

The chalice relates to the element of water.

Pentacle

A pentacle is usually a wooden disk that has a pentagram inside a circle painted or engraved on it. However, pentacles can also be made of metal, clay, or calfskin. The correct name is *panticle*, which means "all angles." However, almost everyone calls it a pentacle, which means "five angles." It is also sometimes called a disk or a shield.

The five-pointed pentagram is the universal symbol of magic. The five points have many associations, including the five elements, the five sacred wounds of Christ, and the head, arms, and legs of a person. The ancient Seal of Solomon was either a pentagram or a hexagram. The symbol has been used for at least four thousand years, and it probably originated in Mesopotamia.

The pentacle symbolizes the element of earth.

Cord

If you choose to wear robes in your rituals, you'll probably have a cord that is tied around your waist. The color of the cord can be chosen to symbolize the main element of the ritual you are performing. If you perform your rituals with others, the colors may determine the ranking of the people involved.

The cord is traditionally four and a half feet long, as this is the radius of a nine-foot magic circle. Consequently, it can be used to mark out the circle that the ritual will be performed within.

Candles

Candles can be found in every tradition. The Roman Catholic, Greek Orthodox, and Russian Orthodox churches all burn candles when making requests. People of all religions, and of none, have used candle magic to effect change and make their wishes come true.

Candles can be selected by color to symbolize the different elements. They should be unscented. Interestingly, all four elements of fire, earth, air, and water are involved in candle magic. An unlit candle represents the earth element. However, when it is lit (fire), the candle starts to melt, creating liquid wax (water) and smoke (air).

You can use as many candles as you wish in your rituals. Traditionally, two candles are used. One, representing the god, or masculine energy, is placed to your right on the altar. The other candle, representing the goddess, or feminine energy, is placed to your left.

Candles usually symbolize the element of fire.

Bell

A bell is sometimes rung during a ritual to ward off evil spirits and to encourage positive energies. It can also be rung to indicate the start and finish of a ritual, and it is often used to mark each quarter (ninety degrees) when casting a circle.

You can use any bell that appeals to you. The bells used most frequently in ritual work are made of brass with a wooden handle. You can buy attractive glass bells, but I've learned from experience that they break too easily.

Other Power Objects

Sometimes you may want to have small containers of salt and water on your altar. These are used when you perform rituals for consecration or purification purposes. The water denotes the water element, and salt symbolizes the element of earth.

If you wish to burn incense to represent the air element, you'll need a thurible or censer. An incense burner can be as basic as a small metal or ceramic bowl. A thurible is a three-legged metal dish. A censer has a cover, and the sides or lid of the container have small holes to allow the smoke to escape. Censers on chains are often swung in high-church ceremonies.

Sometimes deities are used in magic rituals, and small statues can be used to depict these. If you're unable to find a suitable statue, an illustration of the particular god or goddess will work just as well. Today, a huge selection of small statues of deities can be found online.

You may find other items that you can use in your rituals. Feathers, for instance, might symbolize the element of air. A small rock might symbolize earth. Seashells can symbolize water, and orange or red gemstones might symbolize fire. You can use these on their own, or attach them to other objects to symbolize the constant intermingling of the elements.

You might also like to display and use any magical objects that have been given to you or that you have purchased. Several years ago, I was given a beautiful scrying mirror, known as a speculum. It was a piece of glass that had been painted black. An artist had painted Celtic designs around the outside, leaving a circle of glossy black in the center. It stands on a miniature artist's easel. I use it regularly in my rituals. Sometimes it plays a part in what I'm doing. At other times, it's displayed, but not used. I'm sure its energies help all of my rituals, even when it does not have a specific role to play.

Cleansing

When you get a new tool, it must be cleansed, blessed, and consecrated before you use it. This process removes any previous energies that have become attached to the object. Even a new object will have picked up energy during its manufacture. This process also dedicates the object to your magical work. While preparing and using each object, you'll become intimately involved with it. In time, one or more of your ritual objects will become noticeably more powerful than the others, and you'll find yourself using it more and more.

The first step is to examine each object in turn to make sure that it's clean. Dust and dirt should be removed and any imperfections repaired. Sometimes the object might need to be varnished or painted.

Many years ago, I found a coffee table at a church fair. I thought it would make a wonderful altar, and I bought it despite its shabby condition. I had to remove the legs, replace the screws, and sand the woodwork before I could reassemble and varnish it. While doing this, I visualized the coffee table filled to overflowing with my positive energy. The whole process of restoring the coffee table took several hours, but when I'd finished, it looked beautiful. In addition, I'd also established a strong personal connection with it. This table served as my altar for many years.

Consecration

The second part of the process is to consecrate the object(s). Here are three popular ways to do this.

The first method uses the four elements and gives you a taste of what a magical ritual is like. You'll need something to represent each of the four elements. You might use incense for air. However, if this isn't practical, use a feather. You could use a candle for fire, a small container of water for water, and salt or a crystal for earth. You'll also need a table to act as your altar. Place everything you need on the altar. This includes the items you're going to purify, as well as the ritual objects that represent the elements.

Start by having a leisurely bath. Add herbs or bath salts to it, if you wish. The purpose of this is to purify yourself and to become physically and mentally relaxed before performing the ritual.

Once you've had your bath, put on loose-fitting clean clothes. Stand in front of your altar and draw a circle that is large enough to include you and the altar around it. If it's not possible to create a circle, you can simply imagine it. However, it's better if you can mark out a circle, using different objects if necessary to help define it.

Leave the circle, and return again to stand in front of your altar. If you're doing this indoors you may want to leave the room and come back in again.

Face east, and thank the element air for helping you. Ask it to bless the process and to provide you with an abundance of energy.

Turn to the south, and repeat this process for the element fire. Turn to the west and repeat again for the element water. Finally, do the same for the element earth in the north.

Return to your altar and pick up the first item you wish to consecrate. If it's too large to hold perform the process with the object lying on your altar. Allow the item to pass through the smoke generated by the incense. If you're using a feather, pass the feather around the item while shaking it as if it were a brush. At the same time say: "I hereby consecrate and purify you with the element of air."

Pass the item through the candle flame while saying: "I hereby consecrate and purify you with the element of fire."

Sprinkle a few drops of water on the object while saying: "I hereby consecrate and purify you with the element of water."

Finally, sprinkle some salt on the item or touch it with a crystal while saying: "I hereby consecrate and purify you with the element of earth."

Continue doing this with any other objects you wish to consecrate. When you've finished, face each element in turn, starting with earth and moving anticlockwise (widdershins) until you reach air in the east. Thank each element in turn for enabling you to consecrate all of the objects. Return to your altar, snuff out the candle, and leave the circle.

Here's another method that is considerably easier. You can bury the objects in salt overnight, and then let them stand in sunlight or moonlight for a few hours. After this, pick up one of the objects and mentally send some of your personal energy into it. Ask the universal life force to bless the object. Pause until you feel that this has been done. Place the object on your altar and repeat the process with all of the other objects.

A third method is even simpler. Place all the objects on your altar. Stand in front of them with your arms outstretched. Close your eyes and visualize a pure white light coming down from heaven and surrounding you, your altar, and the objects that are to be consecrated. Visualize this as clearly as you can. Open your eyes and gaze at the objects lying on your altar. Say to them: "I dedicate these magical tools to my ritual work." If you prefer, you can use this method to consecrate them one at a time.

Once you've purified your ritualistic tools, you might like to wrap them in silk until you need them. Do not let anyone else handle these tools. They have become part of you and should be used only by you, and only when you're performing a ritual.

Are Any Tools Necessary?

This is a controversial topic. As you know, it's possible to perform any ritual mentally, which means it's performed entirely in your mind. You draw the circle in your imagination and then perform the entire ritual psionically. You can do this anywhere you happen to be. Obviously, you don't need anything except time and imagination.

However, even if you intend doing nothing but mental rituals, I think it's a good idea to collect all the necessary tools. The process of collecting and experimenting with them is an important part of your magical education. Even if you actually never perform a physical ritual, you'll know what the objects look like, and feel like, in your hands. You will be able to imagine them that much more vividly as a result.

seven

Timing

You can perform a magical ritual whenever you wish, but certain times are better than others. If your intent involves some form of manifestation or increase, for instance, the best time to perform it is when the moon is waxing (growing), rather than waning. Whenever possible, work in harmony with the regular rhythms of nature. However, if your need is urgent, you should perform the ritual as soon as you can, rather than waiting for the perfect time.

Invoking rituals, where you want to attract something to you or to someone else, should ideally be performed when the moon is waxing. Good examples of rituals of this sort are invoking good health, confidence, fertility, new beginnings, peace of mind, prosperity, protection, love, and career.

Banishing rituals are performed when you want to repel or end something. Whenever possible, these rituals should be performed when the moon is waning. Good examples of rituals of this sort are banishing illness, anxiety, addictions, anger, pain, stress, poverty, bad luck, loneliness, and negative emotions, such as jealousy.

The Sabbats

Some rituals are performed on specific days. The eight Wiccan solar festivals (called sabbats), for instance, are all held at specific times, and Wiccans around the world celebrate these special days. However, you don't need to be a Wiccan to perform a celebratory ritual on these days. It can be a fascinating and enjoyable experience to experiment with different types of rituals, and you'll learn from every one of them.

The best known of these sabbats is Samhain, or Halloween, which is celebrated on October 31. Here are the eight sabbats that make up the Wheel of the Year:

Winter Solstice or Yule (Approximately December 21)
The winter solstice occurs on the shortest day of the year and marks the start of winter. It's a good day for rituals involving anything you wish to have grow or manifest over the next six months.

Imbolc or Candlemas (Approximately February 2)
Imbolc is also known as Imbolg, Brighid, Candlemas, Oimlec, Candelaria, and Lupercus. It marks the time when

winter is half over in the Northern Hemisphere. Imbolc is associated with Brighid, the fire goddess, and celebrates the approach of spring and everything that this season has to offer. It's a good time for any rituals involving eliminating anything that is no longer needed in your life in order to make room for the changes ahead.

Ostara or Vernal Equinox (Approximately March 21)

Ostara marks the first day of spring, and is sometimes referred to as the spring, or vernal, equinox. Some people refer to it as Lady's Day, as this equinox celebrates the rising of the young god, indicated by sprouting shoots, and his relationship with the Lady, the goddess of spring, who is actually Mother Earth. It's a good time for any rituals involving an increase in health, love, and prosperity.

Beltane or Roodmas (May 1)

Beltane, also known as May Day, is in the middle of spring. It's a good time for rituals involving love and anything else you would like to have more of in your life.

Summer Solstice or Litha (Approximately June 21)

The summer solstice marks the first day of summer, and is the longest day of the year. It's a good time to make plans for the second half of the year and for rituals involving anything you wish to remove from your life.

Lughnasadh or Lammas (August 1)

Lughnasadh marks the middle of summer and the start of the harvest season. It's a good time for any rituals involving letting go of anything that has outworn its use.

Autumn Equinox or Mabon
(Approximately September 21)
The autumn equinox is the first day of autumn. In most of
Europe it marks the time of the grain harvest. It's a good time
for any rituals involving eliminating negativity of any sort.

Samhain or Hallowmas (October 31)
Samhain (pronounced *sow-en, sow* rhymes with *cow*), also
known as Halloween and All Hallow's Eve, marks the middle
of autumn. It's the time when the veil between the world of
the living and the dead is thinnest, and consequently ghosts
and faeries are able to enter the world of the living for a
short while. It's a good time for any rituals that eliminate
outworn addictions, attitudes, habits, and ways of life.

The Four Seasons

The simplest way to time a magical ritual is to use the four
seasons, as they all have associations that can be used in your
rituals. It's unlikely that you'd time your rituals solely on the
season, but they provide useful information that can be used
when you're planning a ritual.

You can use the colors and gemstones listed with each
season in your rituals. These are called "correspondences."
Correspondences are mystical associations between objects
that are believed to be connected, and can consequently be
used to add energy and power to your rituals. You'll find
many more correspondences in the appendix.

Spring

Element: Air

Colors: Yellow, white, and pale green

Gemstones: Aventurine, jade, and rose quartz

Spring is a time of beginnings and new starts. Allow the energy of spring to make you feel positive about your life. Spring is a good time for any rituals involving birth, business, change, and love.

Summer

Element: Fire

Colors: Gold, orange, lilac, pink, red, purple, and green

Gemstones: Amber, carnelian, and citrine

Enjoy the warmth and expansiveness of summer and make use of it in your rituals. Summer is a good time for any rituals involving courage, energy, growth, leadership, love, nurture, and passion.

Autumn

Element: Water

Colors: Blue, bronze, brown, and gold

Gemstones: Amethyst, celestite, and tiger's eye

Autumn/fall is a sign that winter is not far away. Despite this, it's many people's favorite season. Fall is a good time for any rituals involving family, healing, possessions, relationships, and survival. It's also a good time to give thanks for all the blessings in your life.

Winter

Element: Earth

Colors: Black, gray, gold, dark green, red, and silver

Gemstones: Opal, clear quartz, and smoky quartz

Winter is a good time for re-evaluations and for making plans for the future. It's also a good time for any rituals involving death, intuition, meditation, patience, reflection, transformation, and wisdom.

The Signs of the Zodiac

The signs of the zodiac increase the timing possibilities markedly. Here are some of the associations that relate to each sign:

Aries

Dates: March 21–April 20

Element: Fire

Planet: Mars

Nature: Masculine

Day: Tuesday

Gemstone: Diamond

Color: Red

Number: 9

Keywords: I am

Positive traits: Courage and action

Negative traits: Greed and destruction

Suitable rituals: Any rituals involving assertiveness, authority, competition, energy, enthusiasm, initiation, leadership, new ideas, rebirth, renewal, or willpower. Because Aries produces a sudden influx of energy, the best rituals are those that have the potential to produce quick results.

Taurus

Dates: April 21–May 20

Element: Earth

Planet: Venus

Nature: Feminine

Day: Friday

Gemstone: Emerald

Color: Green

Number: 6

Keywords: I have

Positive traits: Affection, patience, and persistence

Negative traits: Aggression and stubbornness

Suitable rituals: Any rituals involving comfort, dependability, finances, grounding, healing, love, loyalty, material matters, patience, persistence, property, protection, reliability, sensuality, stubbornness, or success.

Gemini

Dates: May 21–June 21

Element: Air

Planet: Mercury

Nature: Masculine

Day: Wednesday

Gemstone: Agate

Color: Yellow

Number: 5

Keywords: I think

Positive traits: Affection, communication, and intelligence

Negative traits: Restlessness and shallowness

Suitable rituals: Any rituals involving change of home, communication, creativity, flexibility, friendship, knowledge, public relations, mental stimulation, travel, or writing.

Cancer

Dates: June 22–July 22

Element: Water

Planet: The Moon

Nature: Feminine

Day: Friday

Gemstone: Ruby

Color: Silver

Number: 9

Keywords: I feel

Positive traits: Kind, loyal, and self-reliant

Negative traits: Selfish and unforgiving

Suitable rituals: Any rituals involving emotions, family, femininity, fertility, growing, home, nurturing, protectiveness, or sensitivity.

Leo

Dates: July 23–August 22

Element: Fire

Planet: The Sun
Nature: Masculine
Day: Sunday
Gemstone: Carnelian or sardonyx
Color: Orange
Number: 1
Keywords: I will
Positive traits: Charming, dynamic, and enthusiastic
Negative traits: Egotistical and forceful
Suitable rituals: Any rituals involving courage, fertility, generosity, influence, inspiration, joy, pleasure, power, pride, or strength.

Virgo

Dates: August 23–September 22
Element: Earth
Planet: Mercury
Nature: Feminine
Day: Wednesday
Gemstone: Sapphire
Color: Blue
Number: 5
Keywords: I analyze
Positive traits: Balanced, considerate, and organized
Negative traits: Meticulous and negative
Suitable rituals: Any rituals involving career, dependability, details, dietary matters, discrimination, education,

employment, health, intellectual and practical matters, logic, and self-improvement.

Libra

Dates: September 23–October 22

Element: Air

Planet: Venus

Nature: Masculine

Day: Friday

Gemstone: Opal

Color: Green and Pink

Number: 6

Keywords: I balance

Positive traits: Affectionate, charming, and refined

Negative traits: Arrogant, hurtful, and insensitive

Suitable rituals: Any rituals involving compassion, cooperation, diplomacy, emotional balance, fairness, harmony, idealism, justice, karma, love, or partnerships.

Scorpio

Dates: October 23–November 21

Element: Water

Planet: Mars and Pluto

Nature: Feminine

Day: Tuesday

Gemstone: Topaz

Color: Burgundy

Number: 9

Keywords: I desire

Positive traits: Determined and sincere

Negative traits: Demanding, obstinate, and secretive

Suitable rituals: Any rituals involving desire, emotions, intensity, passion, power, promotion, psychic development, secrets, sexuality, or transformation.

Sagittarius

Dates: November 22–December 21

Element: Fire

Planet: Jupiter

Nature: Masculine

Day: Thursday

Gemstone: Turquoise

Color: Purple

Number: 3

Keywords: I see

Positive traits: Adventurous and independent

Negative traits: Impulsive and self-centered

Suitable rituals: Any rituals involving confidence, higher education, imagination, innovation, integrity, legal matters, philosophy, spirituality, travel, or the truth.

Capricorn

Dates: December 22–January 19

Element: Earth

Planet: Saturn

Nature: Feminine

Day: Saturday

Gemstone: Garnet and lapis lazuli

Color: Silver

Number: 8

Keywords: I use

Positive traits: Disciplined and independent

Negative traits: Critical, insecure, and proud

Suitable rituals: Any rituals involving achievement, ambition, career, discipline, finances, honor, politics, recognition, and status.

Aquarius

Dates: January 20–February 18

Element: Air

Planet: Saturn and Uranus

Nature: Masculine

Day: Wednesday

Gemstone: Amethyst

Color: Indigo

Number: 4

Keywords: I know

Positive traits: Affectionate, intelligent, and modest

Negative traits: Critical, intense, and judgmental

Suitable rituals: Any rituals involving creativity, freedom, friendship, habits, philanthropy, or science. It's a good time for any rituals relating to eliminating bad habits and addictions.

Pisces

Dates: February 19–March 20

Element: Water

Planet: Jupiter and Neptune

Nature: Feminine

Day: Friday

Gemstone: Bloodstone

Color: Blue

Number: 7

Keywords: I believe

Positive traits: Intuitive, kind, and sensitive

Negative traits: Argumentative and selfish

Suitable rituals: Any rituals involving acceptance, the arts, clairvoyance, contemplation, creativity, dream work, intuition, mysticism, and telepathy.

The Quarters of the Moon

The four quarters of the moon play an important role in the timing of rituals. Rituals involving increase, attraction, or to strengthen something should be performed when the moon is waxing (growing). Rituals involving endings, harvesting, banishing, or decreasing should be performed when the moon is waning.

New Moon

The first quarter begins when the new moon is a tiny sliver in the night sky. It's important to determine if it is actually a new moon, or the final stages of the waning moon, as the energy and symbolism are completely different. Fortunately, this is easy to determine in the weather sections of daily newspapers, in astrological calendars, and online. (I use *Llewellyn's Astrological Calendar* and *Llewellyn's Moon Sign Book*, both of which are published annually. When I'm away from home, I use http://www.cafeastrology.com/monthly-calendar.html.)

First Quarter Moon

The first quarter moon is a semicircle, with the right half of the moon visible, and the other half dark. This is sometime referred to as the second quarter moon, so be sure to check your source's terminology.

Full Moon

The entire moon is visible at this stage. This is the most powerful time to perform divinations and ritual magic.

Last Quarter Moon

This is the opposite of the first quarter moon, with the left half visible, and the right half dark. Some sources refer to this as the fourth quarter moon.

Dark of the Moon

This is a two-and-a-half- to three-day period when the moon is invisible as it's close to the sun.

The Moon and the Signs of the Zodiac

The moon passes through all twelve signs of the zodiac in just over twenty-eight days, and it spends between two to three days in each one. You can use the qualities of a particular astrological sign by holding a ritual while the moon is in the sign. However, as there's a slight period at the start and end of the moon's visit to the sign where it is impossible to tell if it's in one sign or the other, it's best not to perform magic until you're sure it's in the sign you're wanting to use.

The Planetary Hours

You can fine-tune your rituals even further by using the planetary hours, as each hour of the day relates to a different planet. As you would expect, there are twelve daytime and twelve nighttime hours. However, these do not relate exactly to the hours as we know them. The twelve planetary hours of daylight are spread from sunrise to sunset, and the nighttime hours start at sunset and last until sunrise. Consequently, planetary hours can be both shorter and longer than the sixty-minute hours we're used to.

Fortunately, it's a simple matter to calculate the planetary hours.

1. The first step is to find out the time of both sunrise and sunset. For the sake of example, we'll assume that sunrise is 7:00 a.m. and sunset is 8:00 p.m.

2. Work out the number of daylight minutes. Between 7:00 a.m. and 8:00 p.m. are thirteen hours, and 13 x 60 = 780 daylight minutes.

3. Divide the minutes by 12 to find the number of minutes in a planetary hour. 780 ÷ 12 = 65. In our example there are 65 minutes in each of the twelve daytime planetary hours.

4. Determine the starting and ending times for each of the twelve daylight hours.

Hour 1: 7:00–8:05
Hour 2: 8:05–9:10
Hour 3: 9:10–10:15
Hour 4: 10:15–11:20
Hour 5: 11:20–12:25
Hour 6: 12:25–1:30
Hour 7: 1:30–2:35
Hour 8: 2:35–3:40
Hour 9: 3:40–4:45
Hour 10: 4:45–5:50
Hour 11: 5:50–6:55
Hour 12: 6:55–8:00

5. The next step is to calculate the nighttime minutes. In our example, there are eleven hours between sunset (8:00 p.m.) and sunrise (7:00 a.m.), and 11 x 60 = 660 minutes. We divide 660 by 12 to determine the number of minutes in each planetary hour. 660 ÷ 12 = 55 nighttime minutes.

6. We can now make a list of the nighttime hours:
Hour 1: 8:00–8:55
Hour 2: 8:55–9:50
Hour 3: 9:50–10:45
Hour 4: 10:45–11:40
Hour 5: 11:40–12:35
Hour 6: 12:35–1:30
Hour 7: 1:30–2:25
Hour 8: 2:25–3:20
Hour 9: 3:20–4:15
Hour 10: 4:15–5:10
Hour 11: 5:10–6:05
Hour 12: 6:05–7:00

7. As these are known as the planetary hours, the final step is to add the planets. These are always listed in a special arrangement, known as the Chaldean or Babylonian order: Sun, Venus, Mercury, Moon, Saturn, Jupiter, and Mars. The ancient Babylonians watched the movements of these seven planets in the sky and listed them in the order that they saw them. They were not aware of Uranus or Neptune, as they're too far away and are not visible to the naked eye.

If the ritual is being held on Sunday, the planet placed in the first planetary hour is the Sun, followed by all the other planets in order.

If the ritual is being held on Monday, the planet placed in the first planetary hour is Venus, followed by all the other planets in order. On Tuesday the first planet is Mercury. Wednesday starts with the Moon, and so on. These planets keep rotating to fill all twenty-four day and nighttime hours. Consequently, if we calculated the hours in our example for a Sunday, the finished chart would be:

Daytime hours:

Hour 1: 7:00–8:05	Sun
Hour 2: 8:05–9:10	Venus
Hour 3: 9:10–10:15	Mercury
Hour 4: 10:15–11:20	Moon
Hour 5: 11:20–12:25	Saturn
Hour 6: 12:25–1:30	Jupiter
Hour 7: 1:30–2:35	Mars
Hour 8: 2:35–3:40	Sun
Hour 9: 3:40–4:45	Venus

Hour 10: 4:45–5:50   Mercury
Hour 11: 5:50–6:55   Moon
Hour 12: 6:55–8:00   Saturn

Nighttime hours:
Hour 1: 8:00–8:55   Jupiter
Hour 2: 8:55–9:50   Mars
Hour 3: 9:50–10:45   Sun
Hour 4: 10:45–11:40   Venus
Hour 5: 11:40–12:35   Mercury
Hour 6: 12:35–1:30   Moon
Hour 7: 1:30–2:25   Saturn
Hour 8: 2:25–3:20   Jupiter
Hour 9: 3:20–4:15   Mars
Hour 10: 4:15–5:10   Sun
Hour 11: 5:10–6:05   Venus
Hour 12: 6:05–7:00   Mercury

The next planet in this series is the Moon, which is the first hour of the following day—Monday.

But if you'd rather not calculate the hours yourself, you can look them up online. (http://www.lunarium.co.uk/planets/hours.jsp is an excellent site for this, and they can create the correct timings for the planetary hours for you, no matter where in the world you may be.)

Once you've worked out the planetary hours for the day you intend doing your magical working on, you can determine the best time of the day in which to do it. Let's assume you have an anger management problem and you want to perform a ritual to eliminate or banish it. You could perform the ritual on a Saturday, which is the day ruled by Mars.

Alternatively, you could perform the ritual on another day, but perform it during the planetary hour of Mars. As this is a banishing ritual, you should also make sure to do it when the moon is waning. In the above example, the best times to perform this ritual on a Sunday would be 1:30 p.m. and 8:55 p.m. If you're a night owl, you could even choose 3:20 a.m. on the Monday morning.

In the next chapter, we'll examine how to choose the right goal or intention for your ritual in greater detail.

eight

Goal Setting and Visualization

There is no point in performing a ritual if you have no goal or intention in mind. Goal setting is hard for most people. If you ask people what they want to be doing five years or ten years from now, most will have no idea. In fact, most people put more effort into planning a summer vacation than they do in setting goals for any other aspect of their lives.

Thirty years ago, I met a young man who fascinated me, as he knew exactly what he wanted to be, do, and achieve in life. Although I haven't spoken to him in more than twenty years, I've followed his career with great interest. He is now a billionaire. He knew what he wanted to achieve, and he went out and made it happen. He's an exceptional person who is a good example of someone who sets goals and then achieves them. Sadly, most people drift through life, as they don't know what they want.

Is there something you've always wanted to attain or achieve? You can turn that into a goal. Be realistic, though. You're unlikely to win a gold medal at the Olympic games if you're sixty-five years old and weigh four hundred pounds. In this case, a goal that involved exercise and better food choices would be more suitable.

Are you facing obstacles? Do you feel hemmed in and unable to progress? Create a goal to overcome these difficulties.

Are you unwell physically, emotionally, or psychologically? Have you been bullied or abused? Create a goal to restore your health, confidence, and self-esteem.

Are there aspects of yourself that you'd like to change? You can transform your life, if that is what you want. Set a goal as the first step to making it happen.

Once you've decided on a goal, you need to take action to make it a reality. A magical ritual will help the process, but it's not a substitute for hard work. Time and effort will still be required.

The medieval Jewish mystics known as Kabbalists considered the intention to be so important to success that they called it the *kavvanah*, or soul of the ritual. The kavvanah is the attitude and state of concentrated focus that Kabbalists consider essential when performing religious duties, such as praying to God. The word *kavvanah* means "directed intention." Without a soul, or kavvanah, to animate and energize a ritual, nothing would occur.

The first step in performing magic is to know exactly what it is you want. Once you've done that, you need to visualize yourself achieving the particular goal. Put as much emotion and energy into the visualization as possible, and experience the outcome as clearly as you can.

You must repeat the visualization on a regular basis, preferably twice a day, for at least two weeks. When I was a teenager, I used to travel to and from work on a bus. I got into the habit of performing my visualizations on the bus, as it was a simple matter to close my eyes and think of my goals while traveling to and fro. The reason I remember this is that another regular passenger asked me about my social life.

"You must be out every night," he said, "as you always sleep on the bus."

Visualization is something you already do many times a day. Every time you daydream, you experience a form of visualization. Think about your favorite teacher at grade school. Can you also see the classroom and the students sitting at their desks? Can you see yourself as you were then?

Think about the person you love the most. Picture this person doing something he or she enjoys. Can you hear the sound of his or her voice? Can you see what he or she is wearing? What about the expression on his or her face?

Think about your work. Can you picture your work area? Can you see the people you work with? If there's a window, can you see what's outside?

These are all visualizations. Some people can actually "see" everything clearly in their minds in glorious color. Other people receive a faint impression. Others experience it in different ways. One person might be better at sensing smells, while another favors his or her sense of touch.

Visualization for magical purposes is almost the same as these. However, when you're visualizing a goal, or a specific outcome, you need to hold the mental picture or pictures for as long as you can. Whenever possible, add emotion to your visualizations, as they help you remain focused longer. Some people like to view their goal as a mini-movie, whilst others see it as a series of pictures. Sometimes one picture may be all that's required.

There's no right or wrong way to do this. Instead of allowing random thoughts to pass through your mind, you focus on the outcome you desire and hold the necessary images in your mind for as long as possible.

Visualizing your goal is the vital first step. Unfortunately, it's also where many people stop. As well as visualizing your goal, you need to do whatever is necessary to ensure it eventuates.

"It's not magic if I have to work, as well," a student of mine complained.

"Could you visualize a brand-new Cadillac in your garage?" I asked her.

She nodded. "Yes."

"Good. Now let's assume you visualize that beautiful car twice a day for a month."

"Uh-huh."

"How long would it take to materialize?"

"I don't know."

"Let's assume it was your goal, and you were determined to make it happen. You visualize it twice a day, and you also work hard to make it a reality. How long would it take to materialize?"

She smiled. "I get it. I can visualize and visualize forever, but if I don't follow up and put energy into achieving it, it's a dream, not a goal."

Many years ago, my wife became friends with a forty-year-old woman who was bringing up three children on her own. Her life was a constant struggle trying to make ends meet. She told us her dream was to work as a hair stylist in the movie industry. However, she had a negative, defeatist attitude.

"I'll never do it, of course," she told us. "I'm too old. I'd have to change location. I'm not glamorous enough. I've no contacts, so it would be impossible to get a start. It's hopeless."

I suggested that she visualize herself as a successful hair stylist working on a major movie production.

"Put energy and emotion into it," I said. "See yourself as clearly as you can, being the very best you can, in the exact position you want."

I was trying to be helpful, but I didn't expect her to follow my suggestions. However, a couple of weeks later when we saw her again, she was noticeably more positive about her life than she'd been before.

"I visualize myself three times a day," she told me. "I'm in a trailer on a film set, and I'm working with some of the top stars in the movies. I'm relaxed and confident, as I know I'm good at what I do. In fact, I'm the best at what I do, and movie companies seek me out, as they want my services. I enjoy chatting with the film stars as I work, and at the end of the day I return home tired, happy, and well-rewarded for my work."

"That's wonderful," I said. "Are you doing anything else to make this a reality?"

Nicola nodded. "I've made a start. I called a TV station to find out how they choose their hair stylists."

"That's good. What did you learn?"

"I discovered that to get a job doing that on TV you also have to apply the makeup. The lady was very nice. She said they had no openings at present, but if I'd send them a CV, they'd keep me in mind." She anticipated my question. "I got my son to help me prepare a CV, and I delivered it personally. The lady I spoke to showed me where they get everyone ready, and I met the two ladies who are doing the job now."

"Is this still something you want to do?"

Nicola laughed. "Even more now. I'm not going to stop until I get my dream job."

Nicola ultimately got the job she wanted. She offered to work part-time at the TV station for no pay, and in return they taught her what she needed to know about makeup for television. Several months later, one of the hairstylists at the station moved overseas to get married, and Nicola was offered her position. She worked there for three years until a major movie company came to her town to make a film. Nicola applied for a position, and she got it.

"The pay is fantastic," she told us. "The only problem is, once the movie is made, I'll have to find another job."

Working freelance in the movie industry is a precarious way to make a living, but Nicola has been doing it successfully for ten years. She doesn't see herself as a magician, but she credits visualization, accompanied by action, for her success.

"I had the dream for many years," she tells people. "But that's all it was—a dream—until I visualized it and made it happen."

Although she may not agree, I think Nicola was also using magic to achieve her goal. I'd love to know if she'd have achieved her goals more quickly if she'd included a magical ritual along with the visualization and hard work.

The Magic of Intention

There is no point in conducting a magic ritual if you have no specific goal in mind. Do you need: more money? Emotional healing? More confidence? A loving relationship? Forgiveness? A better car than the one you drive now? You can request almost anything in a ritual.

You can perform rituals for others, too. You can send healing to others. You can request protection for loved ones who are far away. You can ask for peace in your community and even the world. Until I met someone who does it, it had never occurred to me to send honesty and wisdom to politicians.

Intention is subtly different from goal setting. When you have an intention, you have a particular purpose in mind. You can set an intention for almost anything. You might intend to become fit and healthy again. You might intend to spend more time with the people you love. You might intend to go on an overseas trip, find a partner and have children, or start a new career.

Your intentions can be small or large. It's a good idea to experiment with small intentions first. Your intention might be to have a happy and productive day. Chances are that when you think about the day before going to bed, you'll find that you actually did have a happy and productive day, no matter how many minor frustrations and problems occurred during it.

It's vital for your success to set a specific intention or intentions. This clarifies exactly what you intend doing. Your thoughts shape your reality, and setting a clear intention in your mind causes it to manifest. Naturally, your intentions must benefit everyone involved.

In his book *The Active Side of Infinity*, Carlos Castaneda wrote, "Intent is a force that exists in the universe. When sorcerers beckon *intent*, it comes to them and sets up the path for attainment, which means that sorcerers always accomplish what they set out to do."

As a magician, or sorcerer, you can always accomplish what you set out to do. To ensure success, you need to keep a number of factors in mind:

- You must have a clear picture in your mind of what you want. You have a powerful imagination, and you have the ability to visualize whatever it is you desire. The most important part of achieving your goals is to decide exactly what it is that you want.

- Remember that every thought you have is an intention. Like everyone else, your thoughts are a mixture of positive and negative. Your intention might be to receive a pay raise. However, you might sabotage that intention with your next thoughts. You might think, "With the economy in the state it's in, I'll never get a raise," or, "I'm just a junior member of the staff. I'm not worthy of a pay raise." By thinking in this sort of way, you set an intention and then immediately unset it. Once you set an intention for yourself, you must eliminate any negative thoughts that come into your mind concerning it.

- You must believe in the power of intention. If you don't believe it's possible, it won't happen.
- You must also be unattached to the outcome. This can be difficult, but it is an essential part of the process. If you remain attached to a specific outcome, you limit yourself in many ways. If you remain unattached, you'll sometimes receive something better than you expected.
- You must be prepared to receive. Many people subconsciously feel they are unworthy of all the good things life has to offer. If you feel this may be a problem, visualize yourself receiving the outcome you desire and realizing how beneficial it is for you and everyone in your life.

nine

Preparation for a Ritual

To ensure that your rituals are as effective as possible, you should be thoroughly prepared beforehand. These preparations include choosing a suitable day and time; preparing yourself mentally, spiritually, and physically; and even performing a divination to determine whether or not you should perform the rite.

Divination

It's important to know whether or not you should conduct a ritual. Once you've decided on your intent and know exactly why you're going to perform this particular ritual at a certain time on a specific date, you should perform a divination to find out if you should proceed with it.

You can use almost any oracle you wish. Tarot cards, rune stones, dice, and horary astrology are all good examples. The only oracles you shouldn't use are those that you can subconsciously manipulate, such as the pendulum and clairvoyance. I use my pendulum regularly, but I never use it when I have an emotional interest in the outcome. In situations of that sort, the pendulum gives me the answer I want to hear, which may not be correct.

Sky Stones

You might to like to find your answer using sky stones, sometimes known as "yes-no stones." This is a simple form of Celtic divination that answers questions that can be answered by "yes" or "no." You'll need three stones that are about an inch in diameter: one each of gold, silver, and black. Hematite is perfect for the silver stone, gold pyrite or tiger's eye for the gold one, and obsidian for the black one. These should be available at your local New Age store, and are readily available online. You might prefer to make your own stones by using three river stones and painting them.

These stones symbolize the three thresholds of dawn (gold), dusk (silver), and midnight (black). The ancient druids believed that these three thresholds were times when it was easier to cross over into the otherworlds and receive answers to questions.

Hold the stones in your hand and think of your question. You might ask: "Should I perform a ritual for *(whatever your goal happens to be)* at *(a particular date and time)*?"

Take a few slow, deep breaths and then toss the stones onto a flat surface.

The stone that is closer to the black stone after they've been tossed provides the answer. If the gold stone is closer, the answer is "yes," indicating a positive outcome. If the silver stone is closer to the black stone, the answer is "no." If the stones are an equal distance away from the black stone, they need to be tossed again.

If you haven't experimented with any type of divination tool, you might prefer to ask a professional psychic to perform the divination for you. If you do this, make sure to choose someone who is experienced, rather than a friend who happens to dabble with her tarot cards every now and then.

If you receive a positive response to your divination, you can continue making plans and perform the ritual. It can be disappointing when you receive a negative response, but this forces you to pause and think about why this occurred.

One possibility is that you've chosen a goal that's not in your best interests. A tarot card divination might reveal that, but obviously sky stones can't. A friend of one of my sons planned to give up his teaching career and become a rap singer. He decided to perform some magic to help him make the transition. However, each time he did a divination he received a negative answer. He became angry and performed the ritual anyway. Despite having numerous connections who did their best to help him get established in his new career, nothing worked, and twelve months later he was back teaching sixth graders. He could have saved himself a great deal of stress and aggravation by following the advice he was given in each divination.

Another possibility is that the timing isn't right. Your intention might be excellent, but for some reason, now is not a good time to pursue it. This could be because the universe has an even better opportunity for you, the goal might be good for you but affect others adversely, or you may not be emotionally ready at this stage.

I've found, like my son's friend, that the intention never works out if you ignore the advice given in the divination.

Your Mental Body

Your mental body needs to be prepared before the ritual. Part of this is taken care of by the pre-ritual bath. This allows any tension and stress to be eased away by the warm, relaxing water. You need to feel mentally relaxed and have a sense of excitement and anticipation about the upcoming ritual.

You should determine your goal, or intention, well before the day of the ritual. This gives you time to ask the who, what, where, when, why, and how questions and to perform a divination to determine whether or not you should perform the ritual. Your intention should be written down.

Your Emotional Body

Your emotional body needs to feel calm and relaxed, too. You need to temporarily let go of any emotional problems that are occurring in your life, so that you can focus your mind on the ritual. Any feelings of anger, jealousy, guilt, or anything else need to be dealt with ahead of time to enable you to put all your attention and energy into the ritual. If possible, try to resolve any problems of this sort before the ritual. You may like to create a ritual specifically to solve any emotional issues.

Self-Hypnosis Ritual

One way to eliminate emotional problems is to let them go using self-hypnosis. This is a simple process, and you've already experimented with it in the creative visualization section in chapter 8.

1. Make sure your cell phone is turned to silent and the room is comfortably warm without being too hot. Make sure you won't be disturbed for at least twenty minutes.

2. Sit or lie down, and go through the relaxation process.

3. Once you've mentally scanned your body and determined that you're totally relaxed, imagine that your physical body is morphing into a huge ball of wool. As you look at it, you see various strands leading away from the ball. Each of these strands leads to an emotional issue that you no longer need. Some of these are recent, but there may be some that you've clung onto for many years. Imagine a giant pair of scissors, and visualize yourself cutting off all those unwanted loose strands until the ball of wool is perfectly round. Feel a sense of release and freedom as each strand is cut.

4. Visualize the smooth, round, woolen ball and allow it to gradually transform back to your physical body again.

5. Silently thank the universe for allowing you to be free from all the unwanted baggage that's been holding you back.

6. Enjoy the feelings of peace and freedom for as long as you can, and then silently count to five and open your eyes.

You should repeat this self-hypnosis session again in about two days. The reason for this is that many emotional issues are so deeply rooted that they come back almost immediately. On the second session you'll find fewer loose strands to cut off. Continue repeating this exercise every couple of days until there's nothing left to remove. After this, it's a good idea to have a self-hypnosis session every now and again to make sure you haven't picked up more baggage since the last session.

Another way to release negative emotions is to write them down and then set them free. You can do this by burning them; ripping the sheet of paper into tiny pieces; or even writing your message in invisible ink, turning the sheet of paper into a dart, and setting it free from the top of a hill. Make sure you hold nothing back if you use this technique. No one will ever see what you've written, so you can make it as nasty and unpleasant as you wish. Put as much emotion as possible into the exercise. If possible, write it in the form of a letter to the person who caused your emotional difficulty. Tell this person exactly why you feel the way you do, and then forgive him or her.

I like to place the finished letter into an envelope and put the person's name on the front. I then destroy both the letter and the envelope. Allow yourself to experience a huge sense of freedom and power as you release all the emotional pain.

You need to feel passionate about your intention. If there's no emotion behind it, your results will be minimal. If you find it hard to summon up much emotion, maybe this particular goal is not really that important to you.

Whenever you have a spare moment visualize yourself as having already accomplished your goal. Enjoy the feelings of happiness and satisfaction you now have. Allow as much positive emotion as you can into your visualization.

Your Spiritual Body

You need to feel comfortable with the idea that you are God. In fact, as all of us are part of the universal life force, we can all claim to be God.

In addition to this, as you may choose to invite a deity or deities into the ritual, you need to be able to put your own personality to one side and assume the personality and attributes of the archetype you're temporarily becoming. For a short while you need to become the deity you've chosen.

This is not easy. You need to study the deity, or deities, you've selected, and then think about what they would be like in any given situation. You might even learn about some deities and decide that you wouldn't be able to assume their particular godform. Actors are able to portray roles that are completely different from their normal personality. Most people are not good actors, and if you don't feel comfortable portraying a particular deity, read about other deities until you find ones that you can, temporarily, become.

If the thought of assuming the personality of a deity concerns you, don't do it. Your rituals can be just as powerful and effective using other methods, such as talking to the god within you. If you decide to use archetypal godforms, put everything you have into it. Wear a costume and literally become that deity until you take it off again.

Instead of assuming the personality of a deity, you can temporarily turn yourself into a real magician. To do this you keep your own personality, but add to it all the qualities that you believe a master magician would possess. In effect, you become a more powerful version of yourself. Think about the qualities you'd like this powerful version of yourself to possess. It makes no difference what they are, as long as they can help you achieve your magical goals. In many cases, you'll have to study the qualities you've added to your personality. If this "super" version of you has special knowledge, you'll need to study whatever it is so you can make use of it in your ritual magic.

You might find it helpful to meditate, pray, or perform any other type of spiritual practice before conducting a ritual. As well as being useful in their own right, they also help you get into the required state of mind to conduct your ritual. I like to make a prayer asking for protection of my sacred space.

Your Work Space

It would be wonderful if you had a special space designated solely for magical ritual. I know only a few people who are fortunate enough to be able to do this. Most people have to use a room in their home. Ideally, this should be in a quiet part of your home where you're unlikely to be disturbed. If possible, you should be able to lock the door to ensure that no one accidentally walks in and disturbs you in the middle of a ritual.

You may have to move heavy objects to one side to allow enough room for your circle. You'll also need a table of some sort to act as your altar. Temporarily remove any ornaments or other objects that might prove distracting during the ritual. Remove or cover any clocks. While you're performing a ritual, you're temporarily in a timeless place and you don't want to be reminded of the actual time by suddenly seeing a clock.

The space needs to be cleaned before you can use it. Vacuum or sweep the area while thinking about why you're doing this. Once you've finished, you might be able to sprinkle water and salt over the whole area.

You might also be able to burn some incense to help clear the room of any residual negativity. Experiment with the types of incense you use. I prefer not to use incense, as I sometimes experience an allergic reaction to it. Instead of incense, I imagine the room being cleared and purified physically, emotionally, and spiritually.

Incidentally, if you use incense in your rituals, make sure to turn any smoke alarms off before you start. Leave a note to yourself to remind you to turn it on again once the ritual is over.

Your Altar

Your altar can be as simple as a tray placed on a stool. Small, portable tables are ideal, as they can be moved away once the ritual is over. If you use a free-standing cupboard or bookshelves of the right height, you can use the top shelf as your altar and store your magical tools below. In time, you'll probably want to set up a permanent altar for your magical work. However, a temporary altar will work well until you reach that stage.

In addition to the altar, you'll need a cloth to cover it with. Make sure this is of good quality and looks attractive. I have several cloths of different colors, and I use the color that is most suitable for the ritual I'm going to perform.

You'll also need at least two candleholders (one each for the male and female principles), and you might like to place a small vase of fresh herbs or flowers on your altar as well. If you're going to use incense, you'll also need an incense holder. If you're going to call on a deity, it's helpful to have a small statue or picture of the deity on your altar, too. In addition to this, you'll need the magical tools you'll be using during the ritual.

You can add anything else that you find helpful, such as crystals, amulets, and photographs. However, your altar should not be cluttered with too many unnecessary objects, as you need enough space on your altar to work.

Oracle Tree

I live in a temperate climate and can do my ritual work outdoors at almost any time of the year. Most of this is done beside my oracle tree. You find your oracle tree by hugging trees that appeal to you. The best way is to hug potentially suitable trees as if you were hugging a close friend. Wait for the tree to respond. Sooner or later, one of them will respond in a different way from the others, and this tree will become your oracle tree. I sometimes wonder if I chose my oracle tree or if it chose me. Once a tree becomes your oracle tree, you need to look after the area around it. This includes all the animal and plant life. In return, the entire area will become a special, magical space for you—making it the perfect spot for performing ritual magic.

Ideally, your oracle tree needs to be somewhere quiet and private, where you can work without interruptions or interference.

The concept of an oracle tree comes from the ancient druids. Every clan had a special sacred tree in the middle of their territory. It was devastating and demoralizing if a rival clan managed to destroy this special tree (Webster 1995).

Your Physical Body

You should prepare your physical body by taking a ritual bath before performing the ritual. Although a shower serves the same purpose, a ritual bath is better, as you can relax and mentally prepare yourself while enjoying the warm water. You can also indulge yourself by adding bath salts, herbs, or oils to the water.

You should wear comfortable, loose-fitting clothes during the ritual. Remove any watches, jewelry, belts, or shoes. Many people wear robes, as this enables them to enter an altered state. Some magicians like to work skyclad (nude), as they believe psychic energy flows better when there's no clothing to get in the way. No matter what you choose to wear, the most important factor is comfort.

Bathing

As I said above, one of the things you need to do before starting your ritual is to enjoy a warm bath. Use bath salts or essential oils to help you get into the right mood. Bless the water as you do this. You might like to place four candles around the bath and bathe by their light. Relax and allow the bath to cleanse your physical, mental, and spiritual bodies. It also removes all negativity. Think about the ritual you're about to perform, focus on your intent, and visualize the successful outcome.

Step out of the bath before allowing the water to drain away. Dry yourself with a clean, good quality towel, and dress yourself in the clothes you're going to wear for the ritual. Once you've done this, snuff out any candles you used during your bath, place your ritual tools on your altar, and cast the circle.

Once, many years ago, I took part in a group ritual that was held beside a lake. We were all able to enjoy a ritual bath in the lake. I always think of this whenever I have a ritual bath, as it seemed to me then, and still does now, to be the best possible way to prepare for a ritual.

What to Wear

Many people wear robes that have been made especially for their ritual magic. Many New Age stores have a selection of robes to choose from. The most popular color is black, but other colors, such as purple, red, green, blue, yellow, brown, and white are all readily available. Some people have a number of different colored robes and wear whichever one best suits the ritual they're going to perform. If you prefer, you can make your own or purchase your robes from one of the many suppliers on the Internet. If you choose to wear robes, make sure they're used only for your ritual magic purposes.

You don't have to wear robes. You can wear anything you wish. The only proviso is to ensure that the clothes are clean and loose-fitting. You shouldn't wear clothes that you've worn all day. Change into good quality clothes after your bath. After all, you're going to be contacting deities during the ritual, and you'll want to look and feel your best. You should also remember that changing into special clothes for the ritual is a symbolic act that helps to emphasize the importance of what you're doing. It's best that whatever clothes you wear are used only for your magic rituals. Consequently, you might choose not to wear any clothes that you enjoy socializing in.

Some people like to wear cloaks over their normal clothes. This can be a good idea if you're performing your ritual outdoors on a cool evening.

You can, of course, also work skyclad. This effectively removes all the masks that we wear, and as nudity isn't something most people do in public every day, it psychologically helps everyone involved in the ritual to enter into the right state of mind before the ritual starts. People who work skyclad usually don't wear makeup or jewelry during the ritual.

Now you're fully prepared, it's time to start the ritual. We'll do that in the next chapter.

ten

Practical Ritual Magic

Ritual magic, as its name implies, involves a number of ritualistic actions. These serve a number of functions, including enabling you to enter into the right state of mind to allow the magic to happen. After you've performed several magical rituals, you'll find the actions will become familiar and comforting, and you'll enter into the magical state quickly and easily.

Grounding

The first step is to ground yourself. A large part of magical work begins in the mind, and if you fail to anchor yourself to the ground you might experience "spacey" feelings afterward.

Grounding enables you to gain a closer connection with the earth. It enables you to feel an almost physical connection to the ground. As a highly imaginative child, I was frequently told to "Keep your feet on the ground."

Many years later, when I worked as a psychic reader, I found that keeping myself grounded enabled me to empathize and help my clients without taking on their negativity. For some years, I read palms in shopping malls. These were quick, five-minute readings, and I often read for up to a hundred people a day. That would have been impossible if I hadn't kept myself grounded. Consequently, grounding is useful in many types of situations, and it is a highly useful skill to have.

If you've ever experienced a headache, extreme tiredness, or even nausea after meditating or performing a psychic task, you'll know what is likely to happen if you don't ground yourself before starting the ritual. The grounding allows any excess energy to pass harmlessly into the earth without affecting you. Consequently, the connection you gain with the earth through grounding works in both directions simultaneously. You gain strength, support, and energy from the earth, while at the same time any negative energy dissipates harmlessly into the ground.

In actuality, you ground yourself naturally in your everyday life. Walking barefoot on grass or earth, gardening, and hugging a tree are all good natural ways to ground yourself. You also ground yourself whenever you perform a physical task that you enjoy.

There are many ways to ground yourself. One simple method is to sit or stand comfortably and become aware of your physical body. Mentally scan your body from the top of your head to the soles of your feet. Feel your feet making contact with the ground. If you're indoors, imagine the floor you're sitting or standing on making contact with the ground. I like to wriggle my toes at this point, symbolically making a closer connection to the ground. Imagine that the earth, Mother Earth in fact, is nurturing and supporting you.

Another simple method is to close your eyes and imagine that you're a tree. Your physical body represents the trunk and branches, and you have imaginary roots that extend deep into the earth. This method involves all four elements. The roots are in earth, the trunk and branches are in air, the sap inside the tree is water, and the rays of the sun that nurture the tree are fire.

You can spend as long as you wish on grounding yourself. With practice, you'll be able to do it in a matter of moments, but initially you should allow as much time as necessary to feel that you are totally grounded and have made a strong connection with Mother Earth.

You can ground yourself whenever you feel the need for more confidence, or have to stand up for yourself. If you're not having a good day, a few minutes spent grounding yourself will eliminate negative thoughts and improve your attitude and outlook. You'll also find that your religious or spiritual practices will become more effective if you ground yourself before praying.

Centering

Once you've gained a connection with the earth, you can gain a connection with your inner or spiritual center, which is the source of your own personal power. This process is called centering. Whenever you feel confident, strong, and in control, you are centered. Some people are constantly aware of their bodies' emotional states, and know what to do when they feel stressed, uncertain, and weak. Being able to center yourself will help you develop this ability, if you do not already have it.

We all think that we operate from our own center of power, but this is not always the case. Whenever you rely on someone else's strength and energy, you're operating from his or her center of power rather than your own. To be truly strong and in control, you need to be able to center yourself.

Start by taking some slow, deep breaths. Close your eyes and imagine that with each breath you're sending energy to every part of your body. With each exhalation allow yourself to relax more and more. When you feel completely relaxed focus on a position about two fingers' width below your navel. This is where martial artists summon their power from. As you focus on this spot, allow yourself to feel your life force gaining power and energy in this position before moving through every part of your body, restoring and revitalizing every cell.

If you've always considered your center of power to be located somewhere else in your body, use that position, as it will be right for you. This is because everyone is different. Someone who experiences life largely at an emotional level is likely to have a different center of power than someone who experiences most things at a mental level. Ultimately, we are all connected to the source, no matter where your personal power center might be located.

Wherever your center may be, you might like to place your hands over it to help the visualization. After visualizing your center gaining energy for a few seconds, you'll find yourself becoming peaceful and relaxed. In fact, I do this to help me fall asleep, on the rare occasions when I find it hard to do so. I find it extremely useful on long airplane flights.

Once you're centered, allow the earth energy that you gained from grounding to merge with your centering energy, and visualize it spreading throughout your body and up and out into the universe.

How to Cast a Circle

The circle is a special, sacred place that contains the magical energy that is generated until it's time to release it. As well as containing energy, it also serves a protective function by keeping unwanted energies out. It can be considered a tiny replica of the world, and it is a safe place to work in.

Before casting a circle, the area should be symbolically cleansed with a broom. In the past a woman did this, but today it doesn't matter who does it. If you're working on your own, naturally you'll have to do it yourself, no matter what gender you happen to be.

The circle can be cast in a variety of ways. Some people visualize a pure white light immediately above their head that gradually grows until it forms a circle, or more correctly a half egg, of whatever size they desire. Other people walk clockwise in a circle while clapping their hands or ringing bells to form a circle. The number of people involved in the ritual determines the size of the circle. A traditional Wiccan circle is about nine feet in diameter. Someone working on his or her own needs a circle that is at least five feet in diameter.

If you're working indoors, you might be able to draw a circle with chalk to indicate your sacred space. Alternatively, a circular rug or a sheet of fabric can be used to mark out the circle. Outdoors, you might be able to use a stick or a staff to draw a circle on the ground. Alternatively, you could use pebbles, stones, crystals, flowers, or fallen branches to mark the circle. If you perform your ritual work in a secluded spot, you might be able to construct a permanent circle of stones that are partially embedded in the ground. A permanent circle will gain more and more energy each time you use it. If you're somewhere where it's not possible to create a physical circle, such as a park or at work, you can always visualize one.

Once the circle has been constructed, even if it's a symbolic one, you'll still need to mark its boundaries by walking around it. Most people start in the east and walk around the circle in a clockwise direction.

It's a good idea to chant something as you symbolically draw the circle. This can be anything that relates to the matter at hand. You might like to chant something about the magic you're about to perform or say words that relate to the drawing of the circle. I usually say something along the lines of: "I'm drawing a circle to create a new world. One world within, and one world without. I'm drawing a circle to create a new world." I visualize the circle as I'm doing this.

Some people stop after making a single circuit of their circle, but I like to draw the circle three times. After walking around it to symbolically mark its border, I walk around it again, this time sprinkling salty water. This provides the elements of earth (salt) and water (water) to symbolically cleanse and purify the circle. I then walk around the circle a third time holding a candle or incense. These provide the elements of fire and air.

I have seen people draw the circle five or more times, and this is fine as long as there is a purpose for it. Once I saw all twelve members of a group draw the circle, but they all followed each other with just a couple of paces between each person. Consequently, what could have been a lengthy process was performed quickly.

Fire, Earth, Air, and Water

The elemental symbols of fire, earth, air, and water are credited to Empedocles of Acragas (c. 495–435 BCE), a Greek philosopher, poet, and magician. Sadly, only fragments of two of his works survive. One of these, *On Nature*, gives his account of the universe based on his concept of the four elements. He believed that nothing in the universe came into existence or ceased to exist, and everything was in a state of change caused by love and strife. Plato (c. 428–347 BCE) and Aristotle (384–322 BCE) popularized Empedocles's ideas one century later, and Aristotle suggested a fifth element, which he called *aether*. This was believed to be the air that the gods breathed. Today, this fifth element is often called spirit.

Plato believed that the four elements were intertwined and could easily pass from one to another. He wrote: "Let us begin with what we now call water. We see it, or we suppose, solidifying into stones and earth, and again dissolving and evaporating into wind and air" (Plato translated by H. D. P. Lee 1965). Because of this, Plato felt that the four elements should be considered as qualities that reflect their essential natures.

These elements are much more than the physical substances that bear their names, as the symbolic associations attached to them can be found in every area of life. The four elements symbolize the creative energies, or building blocks, of the universe.

Galen (129–216 CE), the Greek physician and author of *De temperamentis*, based his system of temperaments on the four elements. He believed the perfect person contained a balance of the four elements. Unfortunately, most people contain more of one element at the expense of the others. Galen described these people as "sanguine," "melancholic," "choleric," and "phlegmatic." These relate to different types of personality.

Sanguine people are extroverted, and enjoy spending time socializing and meeting new people. They have good ideas and are often creative. However, they lose interest quickly, and find it hard to finish all the projects they start. Sanguine relates to the air element.

Choleric people are ambitious, passionate, and active. They are often found in leadership roles. Choleric relates to the fire element.

Phlegmatic people are considerate, contented, and loving people who dislike change. They are open, friendly, and accept others for what they are. Phlegmatic relates to the water element.

Melancholic people are sensitive, caring, and independent. They are often perfectionists who like every task to be completed properly. Melancholic relates to the earth element.

All four of the elements are essential for human life. Without earth, we'd have nothing to live on or to grow things in. We call it Mother Earth. We wouldn't last long without water or air. Fire is also essential as it provides heat and the light of the sun. They can be considered the basis of life itself.

You, along with everyone else, contain all four elements in your makeup. Life, itself, is the earth element. The qualities of compassion, emotion, and love come from water. Your powerful intellect and ability to communicate come from air. Finally, your creativity and transformation abilities come from fire. Although everything is a combination of the different elements, in magic the elements are considered individually as symbols that possess their own qualities and energies that can be drawn upon.

There is also the fifth element, postulated by Aristotle. Spirit is said to combine the other four elements to create the universe we live in. Spirit is like a giant spider's web that connects everything.

The five elements are symbolized by the pentagram, which joins all five elements together. The pentagram is often depicted inside a circle. As circles possess no beginning or end, this circle is considered the sacred circle of life.

Magicians found they could use the elements in magic to achieve their goals. Heinrich Cornelius Agrippa (1486–1535) discussed this in his *Three Books of Occult Philosophy*:

"There are four elements … of which all elementated inferior bodies are compounded; not by way of heaping them up together, but by transmutation, and union; and when they are destroyed, they are resolved into elements. For there is none of the sensible elements that is pure, but they are more or less mixed, and apt to be changed one into the other ... And this is the root and foundation of all bodies, natures, virtues, and wonderful works; and he which shall know these qualities of the elements, and their mixtions, shall easily bring to pass such things that are wonderful, and astonishing, and shall be perfect in magic."

Here are some of the symbolic associations, or correspondences, attached to each element.

Air

Temperament: Sanguine

Attribute: Intellectual, fun-loving

Physical sense: Touch

Color: Yellow

Direction: East

Season: Spring

Archangel: Raphael

Tarot suit: Swords (Wands in some traditions)

Keywords: Thought, communication

Astrological Signs: Gemini, Libra, and Aquarius

Air is intelligent, communicative, and restless. It symbolizes reason, intellectual pursuits, language, and the law.

Air is used in rituals relating to addictions, creativity, freedom, transformation, learning, communication, and travel. You can also use air whenever you need encouragement and support.

You can gain your own impressions of this element by going for a walk on a windy day. Notice how you feel, and observe what is going on around you.

Fire

Temperament: Choleric

Attribute: Spiritual, enthusiastic

Physical sense: Sight

Color: Red

Direction: South

Season: Summer

Archangel: Michael

Tarot suit: Wands (Swords in some traditions)

Keywords: Courage, assertiveness

Astrological Signs: Aries, Leo, and Sagittarius

Fire is purifying, energetic, forceful, empowering, and enthusiastic. It is also passionate, sexual, emotional, and potentially destructive.

Fire is used in rituals involving change, competition, courage, energy, health, inspiration, legal matters, loyalty, protection, sex, sport, stamina, strength, and success. You can use fire whenever you need energy and vitality.

You can gain your own impressions of this element by sitting outdoors on a sunny day. Focus on the feelings the warm sun creates on your face, and other exposed parts of your body. Close your eyes, and see what occurs to you as the sunlight caresses your eyelids.

Water

Temperament: Phlegmatic

Attribute: Feeling, nurturing

Physical sense: Taste

Color: Blue

Direction: West

Season: Autumn

Archangel: Gabriel

Tarot suit: Cups

Keyword: Emotions

Astrological Signs: Cancer, Scorpio, and Pisces

Water is soothing, nurturing, receptive, intuitive, and sociable.

Water is used in rituals relating to balance, children, dreams, emotions, family, friendship, healing, home, intuition, love, marriage, peace of mind, and reason. You can also use water whenever you wish to dissolve or eliminate something.

You can gain your own impressions of this element by spending time on a beach or walking beside a stream or river. Pay attention to any thoughts or feelings that come to you as you gaze at the water. If possible, paddle or walk in the water.

Earth

Temperament: Melancholic

Attribute: Physical, security

Physical sense: Smell

Color: Green

Direction: North

Season: Winter

Archangel: Uriel

Tarot suit: Pentacles

Keywords: Practicality, physicality

Astrological Signs: Taurus, Virgo, and Capricorn

Earth is nurturing, stabilizing, grounding, and fertile. It's also patient, harmonious, and honest. Earth is used in rituals relating to abundance, agriculture, career, employment, fertility, financial matters, investments, manifestation, property, prosperity, and wisdom. You can also use earth whenever you need stability.

You can gain your own impressions of this element by spending time in a park or out in the country. If possible, walk in bare feet or sit down on the grass. Notice what impressions come to you as you pay attention to the earth beneath you.

Spirit

Physical sense: Hearing

Color: White or purple

Direction: Center

Keyword: Connection

Spirit symbolizes interdependence, transformation, and change. It also symbolizes truth, spirituality, and love.

You can gain your own impressions of this element by sitting down quietly in a peaceful place. Close your eyes and enter the stillness within. Think about all the people you know: family, friends, work colleagues, and acquaintances. Gain some idea of the number of people you might encounter in an average week, and then think of all the people they might also encounter. Imagine these links spreading throughout the world, and think how we are all interconnected.

The Four Directions

The four directions play an important role in ritual magic. The magic circle can be divided into four quadrants, each relating to one of the elements:

North relates to earth.

East relates to air.

South relates to fire.

West relates to water.

This elemental symbolism was devised by the French author and ceremonial magician Eliphas Lévi (1810–1875). It plays an important role in magical ritual.

Calling the Quarters

Once the circle has been created, you can call the quarters, which involves summoning the four elements. This can be as simple or as involved as you wish. You might like to hold something to symbolize each element as you greet it. Alternatively, you might simply face each direction in turn, greet the elements, and call on them to help the magic and to protect their quarter of the circle. If my circle is large enough, I walk to each quarter in turn to greet them. If there isn't room for this, I simply face each quarter in turn.

Here's an example of how you might greet the quarters:

"Element of air, I greet you. Please provide me with fresh ideas, new ways of looking at situations, creativity, and good communication. Please protect your quarter of the circle. Thank you.

"Element of fire, I greet you. Please provide me with inspiration, intuition, strength, enthusiasm, and energy. Please protect your quarter of the circle. Thank you.

"Element of water, I greet you. Please provide me with sensitivity, empathy, harmony, joy, and love. Please protect your quarter of the circle. Thank you.

"Element of earth, I greet you. Please provide me with patience, stability, perseverance, and security. Please protect your quarter of the circle. Thank you."

The Hermetic Order of the Golden Dawn created the best-known ritual for preparing an area for ritual magic. It's known as the Lesser Banishing Ritual of the Pentagram. We'll look at this important ritual in the next chapter.

The Pentagram

A great deal has been written about invoking and banishing pentagrams, and some people use eight different pentagrams whenever they perform ritual magic. I use one or two. I've been accused of having such a poor memory that I can remember only two. I use the invoking and banishing pentagrams that relate to the element of earth. This is because we start the magic ritual by grounding ourselves in earth, and the earth element relates to manifestation, creation, practicality, and perseverance.

I'll describe all eight pentagrams, as you should experiment and decide for yourself what works best for you. The pentagrams are drawn in the air using your fingers, a wand, an athame, or some other magic tool. You should visualize the pentagrams as you draw them, and continue to see them for a while afterward. I like to visualize them as brightly colored neon signs.

The pentagrams can be small or large. Many people I know draw small pentagrams in front of their chests. However, you can make them much larger, if you wish.

Stand with your feet about shoulder width apart. Draw the pentagram in front of you using your dominant hand (right hand if you're right-handed, and left hand if you're left-handed).

The earth invoking pentagram starts with your hand raised to a point in front of the middle of your forehead. Bring it down to your left knee, up to your right shoulder, across to your left shoulder, down to your right knee, and finally back up to your starting point at the center of your forehead. The earth invoking pentagram can be used for all four quarters.

The earth banishing pentagram starts at the lower left. It goes up to the top center, down to the right, up to the left, across to the right, and finishes by going back down to the lower left. This is the banishing pentagram I use for all four quarters.

The air invoking pentagram starts on the right, and then moves across to the left, down to the right, up high to the center top, down to the left, and finally returns to its starting point on the right.

The air banishing pentagram starts on the left, and then moves across to the right, down to the left, up to the center top, down to the lower right, and finally back up to its starting point on the left.

The fire invoking pentagram starts with your hand raised high. It comes down to the right, up and to the left, across to the right, down to the left, and finally back up to where it started.

The fire banishing pentagram starts at the bottom right, and goes up high to the top center. It then comes back down again to the lower left, up to the right, across to the left, and back down again to its starting point at the lower right.

The water invoking pentagram starts at the left, goes across to the right, down to the lower left, up high to the top center, down to the lower right, and back up to its starting point on the left.

The water banishing pentagram starts at the right, goes across to the left, down to the lower right, up high to the top center, back down to the lower left, and finishes at its starting point on the right.

This may seem like a great deal to learn. In practice, it isn't, as the first line drawn in the invoking pentagram is reversed to create the banishing pentagram. It's best to decide ahead of time which pentagrams you're going to use. Whichever invoking pentagrams you use must be accompanied later by the same banishing pentagram. If you start with the earth invoking pentagram, for instance, you must finish the ritual with the earth banishing pentagram.

Inviting the Deities

Your circle is now complete and you're almost ready to start your ritual magic. The next step is to invite whatever deity, or deities, you wish to have join you in the circle. You may prefer to ask spiritual energy to help you in preference to a specific deity. The deity or energy that you ask to join you is determined by the specific need you have. There may be certain deities that you're familiar with, and would like to work with. If nothing comes to mind, you might choose someone from a book of mythology.

It's not a good idea to select a particular deity at random and then ask him or her to help you. Before you reach that stage, you need to develop a relationship with your chosen deity. You may start out with a small offering of food or flowers. Visualize what your deity looks like. Have an imaginary conversation with him or her. When you feel the time is right, ask him or her for whatever help you need in your magical ritual.

Here are some deities that you might find helpful:

Earth Gods and Goddesses

Artemis is the Greek moon goddess who looks after women during childbirth and protects all animals during pregnancy and infancy. She is willing to help you find new opportunities and resources.

Cernunnos, the Horned God, looks after the underworld, animals, male sexuality, and death. Today, Cernunnos plays an important role in Wicca. Cernunnos provides strength and courage.

Demeter is the ancient Greek Earth Mother and is a symbol of fruitfulness, fertility, and prosperity. She is willing to help in all of these areas.

Freyr, the God of Yule, is called upon for matters relating to prosperity and protection of the home.

Gaia is the ancient Greek Earth and Healing Mother. Her name is frequently used today to refer to Mother Earth.

Gaia is willing to help in any matters that involve abundance, fertility, and the environment.

The Green Man is an ancient European god who encourages the growth of plants. He is willing to help in any matters involving practicality, property, and financial well-being.

Air Gods and Goddesses

Diana, the Wiccan moon goddess, was originally the Greek and Roman huntress goddess. She has been goddess of the witches for at least the last 2,500 years. She is willing to help in all matters involving women, relationships, and healing.

Hermes, the winged Greek god of healing, also helps people achieve their goals and progress in every aspect of their lives.

Jupiter, the Roman god of the sky, rules the universe and is concerned with justice, spirituality, and all matters concerning earth and its inhabitants.

Luna, the Roman goddess of the moon, looks after the moon throughout the year. She is willing to help in any matters concerning love, fertility, and natural health.

Thor, the German god of thunder, looks after thunder, lightning, clouds, and rain. He provides protection and is willing to help in removing obstacles and anything that is no longer necessary in your life.

Fire Gods and Goddesses

Apollo, the Graeco-Roman sun god, also looks after prophecy, healing, poetry, and music. He encourages leadership and fulfillment.

Brighid is the Celtic triple goddess of fire. She is willing to help in matters involving women and creativity.

Ra is the Egyptian sun god who rode his boat across the sky and maintained peace and harmony in the world. He provides energy, fame, and authority.

Sekhmet is the ancient Egyptian goddess of fire, magic, and healing. She is depicted with the head of a lion. She provides women with creativity, power, fertility, and joy. She enjoys helping women succeed in business.

Water Gods and Goddesses

Benten (or Benzai-ten) is the Japanese goddess of the sea. She rides a dragon and plays beautiful music on her harp. She encourages dancing and music, and she also helps reduce pain and sorrow. She can help you let go of the past.

Ganga is the Hindu goddess of water and healing. She helps alleviate pain, sorrow, and suffering.

Poseidon is the Greek god of the sea. He relates to travel and provides energy and power to all creative endeavors.

Write Down Your Intention

Before starting your ritual, you should write down your intention. Ideally, you should be able to write this purpose as a single sentence. If you create an intention that involves several different goals, you're unlikely to achieve any of them. However, if you work on one at a time, you'll find the rituals will generate much more power and energy.

Most ritual magic involves questions about relationships, health, spirituality, and prosperity. Decide which of these areas relates to your intent, and then make your goal as specific as possible.

Writing your intention down helps you to clarify it and forces you to focus on what you want. Once you have the words on paper, you can then ask yourself questions to see if you can clarify your intention even more. Questions starting with who, what, where, when, why, and how can be particularly revealing.

Of course, even after you have your intention and have performed a ritual, you can't sit back and wait for whatever it is you desire to manifest. You need to become actively involved in realizing your goal in your everyday life.

An acquaintance of mine died recently. Every time I met him he complained about his inability to find a girlfriend. Yet he did nothing to help himself. He never socialized or made any effort to meet people. On one occasion, he placed a small advertisement in a newspaper and received fourteen or fifteen replies. However, he didn't follow up on any of these possible leads. In more recent times, he could have tried Internet dating, but he never did, in spite of talking about it endlessly. It's too late now, and he died lonely and unhappy.

If you create a ritual to find a partner, you need to follow this up by accepting invitations, socializing, and doing everything you can to meet new people. The ritual will help you in many ways, but you also need to help yourself.

Not long ago, someone I know moved from a big city where he didn't need a car, back to the smaller city where he had grown up. Jim found work, but didn't have enough money to buy a reliable vehicle. A few days after performing a ritual about this problem, he attended a car fair. He spent a couple of hours looking at different cars and wondering when he'd be able to afford one. Shortly before the fair closed, he started speaking to an older man who was trying to sell his car. The man seemed familiar, and as soon as the man spoke, Jim recognized his voice. He was one of Jim's former high school teachers. The two men chatted for a few minutes about Jim's school days, and then the man said that the car he was selling belonged to his wife. As they were retired, they no longer needed two cars. Jim explained that he'd just moved back to town, and he was looking at cars but couldn't afford one yet. His old school teacher told him that he didn't need the money in one lump sum, and in just a few minutes they came to an agreement that Jim would buy the car and pay it off over a period of time.

If Jim had performed the ritual, but done nothing else, chances are he'd still be catching a bus to and from work. By putting himself in a situation where cars were being offered for sale, he not only found a car at terms he could easily afford, but also made a new friend out of his former teacher.

In the next chapter, we'll look at one of the Golden Dawn's most famous rituals, the Lesser Banishing Ritual of the Pentagram.

eleven

The Lesser Banishing Ritual of the Pentagram

The Lesser Banishing Ritual of the Pentagram, often abbreviated to LBRP, is arguably the most famous of all rituals. It was created by the Hermetic Order of the Golden Dawn in the late nineteenth century, and it was considered so important that all their students practiced it for a whole year before being able to progress further. The LBRP was made public by Aleister Crowley in his book, *Magick in Theory and Practice*.

The word "banishing" in the title means casting out any negativity to ensure that the place you perform your rituals in is full of positive energy and that you're totally protected. Consequently, it's often performed to eliminate any unwanted spiritual energies before performing other rituals.

The process of performing this ritual serves a number of purposes:

1. It eliminates negativity.
2. It provides you with protection.
3. It removes stress and tension.
4. It aligns and centers you to your major intent.
5. It helps you develop your visualization abilities.
6. It increases your confidence.
7. It invokes the divine and temporarily raises you to divine status.
8. It aligns you with the four elements of fire, water, air, and earth, and also fills you with the fifth element of spirit.
9. It brings you into contact with the angelic realms, especially the four main archangels: Raphael, Gabriel, Michael, and Uriel.

The first stage is to enter into a meditative state. The easiest way to do this is to focus on your breathing. Start by taking a slow, deep breath. Hold it for the count of four, and then exhale slowly. Continue doing this for two to three minutes, until you feel quiet, peaceful, and relaxed.

LBRP Part One: The Qabalistic Cross Ritual

The purpose of the Qabalistic Cross is to create a cross of divine light inside your aura. Here is how this ritual is performed:

1. When you feel totally relaxed, stand facing east. (It's best to use a magnetic compass to determine this, as the directions indicated by compasses on cell phones are not always accurate.) Imagine you're standing in the center of an imaginary circle. Extend both arms outward, and then bring your hands upward to your forehead. Place your hands together as if you were saying a prayer. Vibrate or chant the word *Atah* (pronounced *ah-tah*, which means "Thou art"). (To vibrate means to chant the words in a way that makes the air appear to vibrate. Whenever possible, you should perform your rituals using as powerful a voice as you can. This involves taking deep breaths and speaking while you're exhaling. Obviously, if you're performing this rite in your bedroom while the rest of the family is watching TV in the next room, you should vibrate the words silently. If you haven't done any chanting before, you might want to practice by chanting the Hindu mantra *Om* before performing this ritual. *Om*, despite having only two letters, consists of three sounds: *Ahhh-ooo-mmm*. This will help you develop the right feel for the necessary chanting in the LBRP.)

   Visualize a column of white light descending and forming a beautiful white ball of energy immediately above your head.

2. Keep your hands together in the prayer position and slowly lower them until they're at the level of your chest. Vibrate the word *Malkuth* (*mal-kooth*, meaning "the Kingdom"). Visualize a beam of white light

extending downward from the top of your head, through your heart, and continuing downward to the center of Earth.

3. Bring both hands up and across to your right shoulder. Vibrate the words *Ve-Geburah* (*veh-ge-boor-ah*, meaning "and the Power"). Visualize a beam of white light emerging from immediately below your right shoulder and extending outward to the very end of the universe.

4. Move both hands to your left shoulder. Vibrate the words *Ve-Gedurah* (*veh-ge-doo-rah*, which means "and the Glory"). Visualize a beam of white light emerging from immediately below your left shoulder and extending outward to the very end of the universe.

5. Cross your arms over your chest. Vibrate the word *Lay-Olam* (*lay-oh-lahm*, meaning "for ever").

6. Clasp your hands over the center of your chest. Vibrate the word *Amen*.

You have successfully completed the first part, which is actually a complete ritual on its own, by forming a Qabalistic Cross.

LBRP Part Two: Forming the Pentagrams

The LBRP continues by forming the pentagrams like so:

7. Pause for a few seconds and then extend the first two fingers of your right hand to simulate a dagger. You're going to use this "wand" to draw a large,

glowing pentagram of fire in the air in front of you. Visualize it as you draw it. Starting at your left hip, draw an imaginary line up to the top of your head. Bring it back down again to the level of your right hip. Bring it diagonally up across your body to your left shoulder, and then across to your right shoulder. Once you've done that, draw it back down to where you started at your left hip. Finally, charge the pentagram by taking a step forward and thrusting your extended fingers into its center, while vibrating the word YHVH (*Yod-He-Vav-Heh*). Imagine your voice reaching out to the far east of the entire universe. Visualize your pentagram throbbing with energy. Take one step back again.

8. With your arm and hand still extended, turn to face south. Visualize a line of fire following your dagger (first two fingers of your right hand) from the pentagram you've just drawn to the south. Draw another fiery pentagram here, and as you step forward and thrust your hands into its center vibrate the word Adonai (*Ah-Doh-Nai*). Take one step back again.

9. Keep your arm and hand extended as you turn to face west. As before, visualize a line of fire following your hand. Draw a third pentagram, step one pace forward, and "stab" it, while vibrating the word Eheieh (*Eh-Heh-Yeh*). Step back again.

10. Turn another 90 degrees to face north. Draw your fourth pentagram, step forward, stab it, and vibrate the word Agla (*Ah-Gah-lah*). Take one step back.

11. Turn to face east again. This completes the circle. Stand with your feet together, arms extended, and your palms facing upward to create a cross with your body. In your imagination, you should be able to visualize a circle of bright fiery light surrounding you, with four large pentagrams throbbing with energy and power at each quarter.

LBRP Part Three: Evocation of the Four Guardian Angels

LBRP continues by calling the guardian angels Raphael, Gabriel, Michael, and Uriel.

12. With your arms still outstretched, loudly say: "*Before me Raphael, behind me Gabriel, at my right hand Michael, at my left hand Uriel. About me flames the pentagram, and behind me shines the six-rayed star!*" Vibrate each archangel's name, and pronounce them: *Rah-fah-yel*, *Gah-bree-el*, *Me-kah-yel*, and *Oo-ree-el*.

As you say their names, visualize the archangels standing in front of their pentagrams. The archangels are extremely tall and commanding. I visualize Raphael wearing a yellow and purple robe, holding a caduceus wand and a fish, with golden rays of the air element encircling him.

I see Michael wearing chain mail, wielding a large flaming sword, and holding down a dragon with one foot. He's encircled by the red rays of the fire element.

Gabriel holds a trumpet, wears blue and orange robes, and is encircled by blue rays of the water element.

Uriel holds sheaves of wheat and wears robes of olive, brown, and green. He is encircled by the green rays of the earth element.

As you say "behind me shines the six-rayed star!" visualize above and below you a huge golden hexagram, the six-rayed star. The six-rayed star indicates the ideal state of consciousness you should be in when performing ritual magic. The six-rayed star is comprised of two overlapping triangles, one pointing upward and the other down. The downward pointing triangle indicates your Higher Self perfectly balanced with the upward pointing triangle which indicates your Lower Self.

LBRP Part Four:
The Qabalistic Cross Repeated

To complete the LBRP, repeat the Qabalistic Cross.

13. Hold the visualization in your mind for as long as you can.
14. Repeat Part One: The Qabalistic Cross.
15. You are now totally protected and ready to proceed with your own magical ritual.

LBRP Notes

This ritual invokes the divine into every part of your mind, body, and soul, making you temporarily divine. It provides you with limitless strength and confidence. The fiery pentagrams not only provide protection, but invoke spirit, which is the fifth point of the pentagram. This can be visualized as a column that completely fills you and the circle you created, and continues both above and below you into infinity. Once you have done this ritual, you are completely protected and are able to proceed with whatever your intent happens to be.

There are many variations of the LBRP, and once you know it well you might wish to make a few adjustments of your own, too. You'll find, for instance, that many people perform this ritual using their right hand, rather than both hands. (Left-handed people should use their left hand.) Experiment to find which method works better for you.

Crowley wrote that the pentagrams should be visualized as flaming. However, many people feel the pentagrams should be visualized as bright blue or white light (Cicero and Cicero 2003). Again, you should experiment to see which is better for you.

Instead of using your fingers to replicate a dagger or sword, you might choose to use an athame or knife. It's important that this knife has been purified and consecrated for its purpose and has not been used to kill anything. After performing the LBRP with it, it can't be used for any mundane task, and it must be kept solely for magical purposes.

You may also like to visualize the six-rayed star behind you, with the lower point at the base of your spine and the upper point at the level of the top of your head.

Uriel is sometimes spelled Auriel. If you prefer this variation, you should pronounce Auriel as *Aw-ree-ell*.

You're well on the way to becoming a ritual magician. In the next chapter, we'll create a sample ritual to enable you to see how everything we've discussed so far is used.

twelve

How to Create a Ritual

N ow that we've covered everything you need to know to perform a complete ritual, it's time to learn how to create a ritual for yourself. It's possible to obtain ready-made rituals for a variety of purposes, but I've never used them, as I feel an important part of the process is to think about the ritual I'm going to perform ahead of time. Creating your own rituals is a good way to do that.

Step One: Intention

Let's assume you feel lacking in confidence and wish to create a magical ritual to feel confident in every type of situation. The first step is to write down your intention. You might write, "I want to be more confident." If you're lacking confidence in all areas of your life, that might be all you need. However, most people feel confident in certain parts of their lives, but would like additional confidence in other areas. Let's assume you feel confident at work and when you're with family and close friends, but find social situations hard to deal with. After thinking about this, you might change your intention to read: "I want to feel confident in social situations." An hour or so later, you might realize that you feel confident in some social situations, such as when you're accompanied by a friend or two, or if the group includes people who share similar interests to you. You might change your intention to: "I want to feel confident when meeting people for the first time." You can continue modifying and fine-tuning your intention until it says exactly what you need.

Step Two: Creative Visualization

Once you have your intention, you can perform a creative visualization exercise to see what your life will be like once you've achieved your goal. You already know how to do a creative visualization, as you do this every time you daydream. For instance, you might be at work and wish you were enjoying a vacation on a tropical island. Instantly, pictures will come into your mind. You might see yourself relaxing on the golden sands of a beautiful beach. You might be swimming in the warm waters of a tropical lagoon or drinking a piña colada while relaxing by the pool at your luxury resort hotel. If you've been to this particular place before, memories will return and you'll be able to relive them in your mind. You'll continue daydreaming until something disturbs you or you decide to bring yourself back to reality.

Daydreams aren't planned, though. You go in and out of them all day long. For the purposes of your ritual, you need to do a controlled creative visualization. You need about twenty minutes of uninterrupted time to do this.

Sit down in a comfortable chair or lie down on the floor. I don't do this on a bed, as I usually fall asleep if I get too comfortable. Make sure the room is warm enough, but is not too hot. You might like to cover yourself with a blanket.

Close your eyes and take three slow, deep breaths. As you exhale, silently say "relax, relax." Once you've done this, you can forget about your breathing and focus on the toes of your left foot. Allow them to relax as much as they possibly can. When they feel totally relaxed, allow the relaxation to spread into your foot. Once it feels completely relaxed, repeat the process with the toes of your right foot, and then allow the relaxation to drift into the foot itself. Once your right foot feels relaxed, allow the relaxation to drift into your ankle, calf muscles, knee, and thigh. Take as long as you necessary to allow your entire right leg to feel completely relaxed. Repeat this process with your left leg.

Once both legs feel totally relaxed, allow the relaxation to gradually move up into your abdomen, stomach, chest, and shoulders. Allow the relaxation to drift down one of your arms and then into your hand and fingers. Once they're fully relaxed, repeat this with your other arm.

Allow the relaxation to move up into your neck, face, and scalp. Pay special attention to the fine muscles around your eyes.

You are now completely relaxed. Confirm this by mentally scanning your body. If any areas still contain a degree of tension focus your attention on them until they dissolve and relax. Once you're sure that every part of your body is totally relaxed, you can start the creative visualization.

The first part is to remember a situation in which whatever it is you are trying to do was absent. In our example, you'd think of a time when your confidence let you down or you failed to act in a confident manner. Picture this scene in your mind as if it were on an old black-and-white television set. Everyone is different. You might be able to "see" it clearly in your mind. You might see it faintly, or not at all. You might hear sounds or relive the feelings you had at the time. It makes no difference how you experience it. Once you have the scene in your mind, tell yourself that it belongs in the past and allow it to become smaller and fainter until it disappears.

Now allow yourself to experience the scene again, but this time see it all in glorious color. Picture yourself with all the confidence in the world. See yourself talking to people, feeling relaxed and totally at ease. Allow this second scenario to grow as large as possible until it seems as if you're watching it on a huge movie screen. Tell yourself that this is how you're going to be from now on whenever you find yourself in that type of situation.

Enjoy the second scene for as long as you wish. When you feel ready, let it go, and tell yourself that you'll open your eyes at the count of five, and will feel fine and relaxed. Wait for a few moments, then slowly count to five. Open your eyes, become familiar with the room you're in, stretch, and get up.

Have something to eat or drink after this, as this helps you to ground yourself again after the visualization.

Step Three: Write a Script

Some people do little planning before performing a ritual. They may have a standard start and finish that they use for every ritual, but the most important part is left to chance. I prefer to write a script. This ensures that I cover everything, and I don't accidentally leave anything out. I seldom follow the script word for word, but I keep it with me to refer to while I'm performing the ritual. I strongly suggest that you write a script, too.

There are a few things you need to keep in mind while writing your script:

1. You need to keep your intention at the forefront of your mind, both while writing the script and also while performing the ritual.

2. Keep it as simple as possible. It's common for people who are writing their first scripts to make them too involved and to use a great deal of archaic language. A simple script that everyone can follow is easier to write and perform than something that's long and confusing.

3. Keep it short. Because you want to hold everyone's interest and attention throughout, you should eliminate anything that's not necessary for the success of the ritual.

4. Pay attention to the details. Write down everything that is required and needs to be done at every stage of the ritual.

5. Practice. This is something you won't find in many books. I feel it's important to run through the ritual as many times as possible before performing it. Each time you do this, you're likely to make slight changes to your script. You might change your wording to improve what you've written.

As well as reading through the script, you should also hold a number of "dress rehearsals" to make sure everything is in place and runs smoothly. Lay out everything that you're going to need, put on the clothes that you're going to use, and act out the entire ritual. Practicing the ritual also helps you learn your lines, so you won't need to refer to your script as often. The dress rehearsals might also cause you to change your script as you think of better ways to express what you mean. Add drama to the ritual. It's better to practice your gestures and movements ahead of time to ensure that they fit in with the intention of the ritual. I'm convinced some people like rituals mainly because it's an opportunity to dress up and act out a role. This is all very well, but try not to overact.

6. Keep your sense of humor. Obviously, rituals are conducted for serious concerns. However, it's always a good thing to inject some humor into the proceedings, if possible. It's not the right time for a series of jokes, but a funny line or two will help lighten

what might otherwise be an overly serious business. You also need to keep your sense of humor while performing the ritual. Mistakes will occur. Someone might unintentionally say the wrong thing. I vividly recall a "wardrobe malfunction" at a ritual I attended some years ago. Fortunately, the woman concerned took it in her stride and laughed along with everyone else.

7. You might be the person writing the ritual, but if there are other people involved, you may not necessarily be the star. Remember to give everyone involved a chance to do something that's relevant to the ritual. It can be incredibly boring to stand in a circle doing absolutely nothing while one person monopolizes the proceedings. If you're practicing solitary magic, this doesn't apply, of course. However, even if most of your rituals are performed on your own, every now and again you may have to write rituals that involve two or more people. I find that, even when writing solitary rituals, I look for opportunities for other people to do something important. This makes it easier for me to convert them to group rituals if the opportunity occurs, and it also helps when I write rituals that involve a number of people. Writing group rituals is much like writing a play, and everyone needs to have a part in it.

8. Your rituals should benefit everyone. Make sure when writing your rituals to focus on the positive. You might have strong feelings about something, but you need to ensure that no nastiness or vindictiveness

comes into your script or ritual. If you have doubts about something you've written, ask yourself if it benefits everyone concerned. If there's the slightest possibility that someone could be hurt or offended, eliminate it. Your rituals should be life-affirming and focus on what is good and true.

Before You Start to Write

Before you sit down to write your ritual, there are a number of things that need to be considered. Like many people, I sometimes get an idea and immediately start working on it without gathering all the information I need first. I've found out the hard way that it's much easier to write a suitable ritual if I pause for long enough to answer a few questions first.

Let's assume you've moved to a new location and your intent is to make new friends. Based on this intent, you decide to perform the ritual on a Friday with a waxing moon, as this is Jupiter's day. If that's not possible, you'll perform the ritual during the hour of Jupiter on another day.

1. The first step is to decide which gods and goddesses, if any, you wish to involve. You think Zeus, Jupiter, Isis, and Venus would all be suitable choices. Let's assume, that after reading as much as you can about them, you decide to ask Jupiter and Venus for assistance.

2. As pink relates to friendship and love, you might decide to use pink tourmaline in the ritual. You could also choose lodestone, as it is a natural magnet that will help you attract friends.

3. Where will you hold the ritual? As you're new to the area, you might decide to hold it in your living room.

4. How many people will be involved in the ritual? You know very few people in town and don't want to involve anyone else. If this is the case, you'll write the ritual for just one participant—you.

5. Are there any ethical concerns? Could this ritual adversely affect anyone? Hopefully, you won't be able to think of any negativity that could result from your ritual.

6. What physical preparations need to be made? If you're doing this in your living room, there probably won't be much that needs to be done. A few items of furniture might need to be moved out of the way and the altar would need to be placed in the center of the room. You'll need to remove anything that could be distracting, such as family photographs, and you'll also need a broom to sweep your sacred space.

7. How will you set the mood? Candles, music, poetry, incense, or something else? After thinking about this, you might decide to light some candles and play some quiet meditation music.

8. What magical tools will you use? What other objects will you use for this ritual? You decide to use tools to symbolize all four elements, two small figurines to represent Jupiter and Venus, and a photograph clipped from a magazine showing a group of friends having a good time together.

9. What will you do immediately after the ritual is over? You decide on the particular food and drink you'll consume. You also decide how you can transform your sacred space back into your living room once again.

10. When will you perform a divination? You shouldn't proceed any further until you've conducted a divination to determine the outcome if you proceed with the ritual.

Starting to Write

Everything you're planning to do needs to be recorded, and this includes the preparations. I write these in the form of a checklist that I can mark off as each one is completed. For this ritual, the checklist might look like this:

Required
- Two white candles
- Four additional candles: one each of red, green, blue, and white
- Matches
- Candlesnuffer
- Illustrations of Jupiter and Venus
- Athame, wand, quartz crystal, and chalice
- Altar

Preparations
- Choose the space where the ritual will be performed.
- Clean the area where the ritual will be held.

• Define the space. (You might use a length of cord or rope to mark out a circle. You might be able to mark it with chalk. When working indoors, I usually use a circular rug that defines the size of my magic circle.)

• Place the altar in position, and set it up. (You might cover your altar with a blue or violet cloth to symbolize Jupiter. Place two white candles, ritual tools, intent, and anything else you might need, on your altar.)

• Place the four additional candles in position: a white candle in the east of your magic circle to represent the element of air, a red candle in the south to represent fire, a blue candle in the west to represent water, and a green candle in the north to represent earth.

• Bathe.

• Put on robes. (If you don't have specific ritual garments to wear, you might work skyclad, or dress in clean clothes. Ideally, whatever you wear should be worn only when performing rituals.)

A Sample Ritual

Walk into the circle and stand in front of the altar facing east. Take three slow, deep breaths, and then walk to the white candle in the east. Kneel down and light it. Stand up, spread your arms, and say: "I call on all the powers of the east to protect this sacred space and help me perform this rite." Take three slow, deep breaths while gazing out to the east.

Walk to the south, kneel down, and light the red candle. Stand up, spread your arms, and say: "I call on all the powers of the south to protect this sacred space and help me perform this rite." Take three slow, deep breaths while gazing out to the south.

Walk to the west, kneel down, and light the blue candle. Stand up, spread your arms and say: "I call on all the powers of the west to protect this sacred space and help me perform this rite." Take three slow, deep breaths while gazing out to the west.

Walk to the north, kneel down, and light the green candle. Stand up, spread your arms and say: "I call on all the powers of the north to protect this sacred space and help me perform this rite." Take three slow, deep breaths while gazing out to the north.

Return to your altar and face east. Spread your arms with palms raised, gaze upward, and say: "I call upon the universal spirit to protect this sacred space and help me perform this rite." Take three slow, deep breaths, and then look downward. Say: "I call upon Mother Earth to protect this sacred space and help me perform this rite."

Lower your arms, and visualize a stream of white light coming from above, filling you and your protected circle with divine love and peace. Say: "I am surrounded and protected, above and below, and all around. Thank you, powers of the east, south, west, and north. Thank you, universal spirit. Thank you, Mother Earth." As you say that, move to face each direction in turn.

Turn back to your altar and light the two white candles. Walk in a clockwise direction around your circle three times. This generates a vortex of energy inside the circle. When you return to your altar say: "My circle is full of divine energy and power. I have everything I need to accomplish this rite.

Extend your arms and turn around in a complete circle. Pick up your intention and read it. "I wish to make good friends in *(name of place)*. I am prepared to be a good, supportive friend in return, and I am happy to make the first steps toward establishing good relationships with others."

Place your intention back on the altar. Pick up whatever you're using to represent Jupiter. Hold it in both hands at eye level. "Jupiter, great god of the Romans, I ask you to help me make friends here in *(name of place)*. I've been here only a short while. I like it here, but it would be so much better if I had a friend. Please help me."

Replace Jupiter on your altar. Pick up whatever you're using to represent Venus and hold it in both hands at eye level. "Venus, great goddess of love, I ask you to help me make friends here in *(place)*. I love people, but I've been here only a short while, and have not yet made a friend. I like it here, but my life would so much better if I had a friend. Please help me."

Replace Venus on your altar. Pick up the crystal (pink tourmaline or lodestone). Hold it high above your head. Face east and say: "Great powers of the east, please imbue this crystal with energy to attract the right people to me, people who'll become good friends. Thank you."

With the crystal still above your head, turn to the south and say: "Great powers of the south, please imbue this crystal with energy to attract the right people to me, people who'll become good friends. Thank you."

Turn to the west and say: "Great powers of the west, please imbue this crystal with energy to attract the right people to me, people who'll become good friends. Thank you."

Turn to the north and say: "Great powers of the north, please imbue this crystal with energy to attract the right people to me, people who'll become good friends. Thank you."

Still holding the crystal above your head, look up and say: "Universal energy, please imbue this crystal with energy to attract the right people to me, people who'll become good friends. Thank you."

Lower the crystal to your waist. Look downward and say: "Mother Earth, please imbue this crystal with energy to attract the right people to me, people who'll become good friends. Thank you."

Turn back to face east and hold the crystal in your cupped hands. Visualize it full of energy and power. Feel in every fiber of your being that this empowered crystal will help you attract good friends.

Place the pink tourmaline back on the altar. Pause, and then speak sincerely to the images of Jupiter and Venus.

"Jupiter, great god of the Romans, thank you for listening to my intent and for helping make it real. I appreciate your strength and support.

"Venus, great goddess of love, thank you for listening to my intent and for helping make it real. I appreciate your strength and support."

Turn to the east and say:

"Thank you, great powers of the east, for guarding and protecting this sacred space. I am very grateful."

Turn to the other three quarters in turn, and say:

"Thank you, great powers of the south, for guarding and protecting this sacred space. I am very grateful.

"Thank you, great powers of the west, for guarding and protecting this sacred space. I am very grateful.

"Thank you, great powers of the north, for guarding and protecting this sacred space. I am very grateful.

Turn to face east again. Look upward and say:

"Thank you, universal spirit, for guarding and protecting this sacred space. I am grateful for everything you do for me each and every day. Thank you."

Look downward and say:

"Thank you, Mother Earth, for guarding and protecting this sacred space. I am grateful for everything you do for me, each and every day. Thank you."

Snuff out the two candles on the altar. Snuff out the candles marking the quarters, starting with the white candle in the east, followed by the candles in the south, west, and north.

Pick up the pink tourmaline and leave the circle. The rite is over.

Afterward

- Wrap the crystal in a silk cloth and place it somewhere safe.
- Eat a handful of nuts and raisins. Drink some green tea.
- Put away all the items that were used in the ritual.
- Think about the ritual, and record any thoughts you may have in a journal. Add any additional thoughts that occur to you over the next week or two.
- Repeat the ritual as often as necessary.

• Accept as many invitations and opportunities as possible.

Here are two sample scripts for a confidence-boosting ritual. The first one is a mental ritual, where everything happens in your mind. Consequently, there's no need for candles, bells, athames, or even an altar. This ritual does not call on a deity, either.

Ideally, this ritual should be performed on a Sunday, with a waxing moon, as the sun relates to confidence issues.

All you need do is sit down somewhere, relax, and in your imagination see yourself going through the following stages of a ritual:

1. Sweep the area where the circle will be cast.

2. Cast the circle.

3. Leave the circle and reenter it.

4. Call the quarters, using either the invoking or banishing earth pentagram. You may prefer to do the LBRP.

5. Raise both arms over your head and, starting in the east, slowly turn in a complete circle until you are facing east again. Lower your arms.

6. Face east, close your eyes, and relive the second part of your visualization—the colorful one on the huge movie screen where you had all the confidence in the world. Repeat this facing south, west, and north in turn.

7. Face east again and ask for the confidence you need. "Guardians of the east, please grant me confidence when meeting new people. Please give me the abil-

ity to communicate with others effectively in a calm and relaxed manner. Thank you."

8. Turn to face south and say: "Guardians of the south, please grant me confidence when meeting new people. Give me confidence, motivation, positivity, and intelligence. Thank you."

9. Turn to face west and say: "Guardians of the west, please grant me confidence when meeting new people. Give me empathy, friendship, energy, and inner strength. Thank you."

10. Turn to face north and say: "Guardians of the north, please grant me confidence when meeting new people. Give me gentleness, patience, understanding, and good relationships with others. Thank you."

11. Face east and relive the second part of your visualization again. Say a sincere thank-you to the guardians of the east. Repeat with south, west, and north. As you say your thanks believe with every fiber of your being that this is going to be your reality from this time on.

12. Face each quarter and perform the banishing pentagram.

13. Leave the circle feeling totally confident that your desire will manifest.

14. Take a few slow, deep breaths and open your eyes. Get up and have something to eat and drink. This grounds you and helps bring you back to your regular, everyday world again. This is often called "cakes

and ale." I usually eat fruit and nuts, and never turn down wine.

It's an interesting experience to perform an entire ritual in your mind. Many people find it hard to focus and concentrate long enough to do it. The big advantage mental rituals have over physical rituals is that they can be performed quickly and easily, as very little preparation is required. Some people perform nothing but mental rituals, while others never use them. I use both, and I decide which type to do when planning the ritual.

The celebrated British occultist and author Dion Fortune (1890–1946) and fellow members of her group, the Fraternity of the Inner Light, performed rituals of this sort during the bombing of London during World War II (Richardson 2009).

Here's an example of a physical confidence-building ritual.

Time: Sunday, waxing moon (or any other suitable time)

Required: An altar, athame, wand, chalice containing water, pentacle or a piece of crystal, a red candle, bell, salt, and water

In addition, you'll need some items that have correspondences with confidence. I usually use herbs and gemstones, but you should use anything that feels right for you. Anything red or orange would work well. I'd probably choose heather and/or rosemary for the herbs, and agate, aventurine, bloodstone, carnelian, citrine, diamond, garnet, lodestone, rose quartz, ruby, tiger's eye, or tourmaline for the gemstone.

1. Sweep the area where the circle will be cast.
2. Place the altar in position in the center. Place all the necessary items onto it.

3. Cast the circle.

4. Leave the circle and reenter.

5. Call the quarters using your wand and the invoking pentagram.

6. Raise both arms in a V, and slowly turn in a complete circle starting and finishing facing east. Lower your arms.

7. Pick up the bell and walk around the perimeter of your circle. Pause at each of the cardinal points and ring the bell. Ring it again when you return to your altar. (The bell's cheerful sound helps raise the energy inside the circle.)

8. Pick up your athame and hold it high as you face east. "Guardians of the east, please grant me confidence when meeting new people. Please give me the ability to communicate with others effectively in a calm and relaxed manner. Thank you."

9. Replace the athame on your altar and pick up your wand. Face south, raise the wand, and say: "Guardians of the south, please grant me confidence when meeting new people. Give me confidence, motivation, positivity, and intelligence. Thank you."

10. Replace the wand on your altar and pick up your chalice. Face west, hold the chalice high in both hands and say: "Guardians of the west, please grant me confidence when meeting new people. Give me empathy, friendship, energy, and inner strength. Thank you."

11. Replace the chalice on your altar and pick up the pentacle or crystal. Face north, hold the pentacle up high, and say: "Guardians of the north, please grant me confidence when meeting new people. Give me gentleness, patience, understanding, and good relationships with others. Thank you." Replace the pentacle on your altar.

12. Light the candle. When it's fully alight, pick it up and gaze into the flame for several seconds. Repeat the following words several times: "I am confident. I have all the confidence I need." Replace the candle on your altar.

13. Pick up the item or items you've chosen to symbolize confidence. It might be an herb, a gemstone, or something else that has a correspondence to confidence in your mind. Starting in the east, hold up the items, and ask the guardians to imbue the objects with confidence, so that they can provide you with instant confidence whenever you need it. Pause for ten seconds, and then say "thank you." Face the other three directions in turn and repeat this request and thanks. Replace the items on your altar.

14. Starting in the east, face all four directions and give sincere thanks to the guardians for giving you the confidence you need. Each time you say "thank you," believe with every fiber of your being that this is going to be your reality from now on.

15. Face each quarter and perform the banishing pentagram with your wand.

16. Snuff out the candle, and leave the circle feeling totally confident that you'll have all the confidence you need from this moment on. (Never, ever leave the circle with your candles still alight. Many years ago I saw a tent destroyed in a matter of seconds after a ritual when an unattended candle set it on fire.)

17. Ground yourself by eating and drinking something. I usually eat fruit and nuts accompanied by a glass of wine.

18. Place the items you used to symbolize confidence somewhere safe. If they're small enough to carry in your pocket or purse, you can use them as charms and amulets to attract confidence everywhere you go. Whenever you see or touch them, they'll remind you that you have all the confidence you need.

thirteen

After the Ritual

You're likely to feel energized and exhilarated for a while after performing a formal ritual. Allow as much time as necessary to return to your normal self before starting any other tasks. If I've performed a ritual in the evening, I like to read something light for thirty or forty minutes before getting ready for bed. If I've performed my ritual during the day, I enjoy a leisurely cup of tea with a handful of nuts before carrying on with the day. These are the rituals I use to help me unwind after performing any ritual magic.

You might choose to go for a walk, listen to music, make love, have a long shower or bath, play computer games, or enjoy a conversation with a friend or family member. It doesn't matter what you do, as long as you ground yourself again and return to your everyday life.

Obviously, you'll unwind in a different way if you're participating in a group ritual. Usually, the people taking part enjoy eating and drinking together after, or sometimes during, the ritual. This enables the participants to get to know each other better and to discuss the ritual they've all performed.

I also express gratitude to the universe for all the blessings in my life. I have a strong sense of anticipation that everything will work out and that my ritual will achieve the results I want.

Once all the excitement and energy that built up in my mind and body during the ritual have returned to normal, I'll consciously let go of my intent, as I feel confident that the universe will work on my behalf and make it happen. It may seem strange to put all the required work into a ritual, and then, once it's over, simply let the intent go. However, there is a reason for this.

Divine detachment is the state of observing something from the viewpoint of the soul, and being prepared to accept whatever outcome eventuates. It could be described as looking at the "big picture." Obviously, while I'm waiting, I remain totally convinced that the desired result will occur. I'll go about my life in my normal way, but at odd moments during each day I'll allow feelings of positivity and joy to fill every cell of my body as I think about my intent.

If the desired results don't come as quickly as I'd like, I'll think about every aspect of the ritual and how it could be improved. If necessary, I'll perform this revised version of the ritual, and I will continue doing this for as long as necessary.

Of course, there'll be times when a ritual doesn't appear to work. You might have a serious intent and have done everything you thought necessary to ensure a positive result. Some people justify this lack of success by saying, "The universe is still working on it." This is, of course, a possibility, but I feel it's an unlikely one. It's more likely that you've achieved partial success, rather than have nothing whatsoever to show for the ritual. Sometimes the results are hard to measure. If your ritual related to increased confidence, for instance, a slight improvement might not be noticed initially.

It's possible that you didn't have the right attitude or weren't in the right frame of mind when performing your ritual. You may have had doubts that it would work. You may have performed it in a half-hearted way, with little or no energy put into it. Conversely, you may have been overly confident. You can't demand results. You can ask, but you can't insist.

Another possibility is that you failed to do anything to help the process. The law of attraction works, but only if you start actively working toward your goal. You can't, for instance, ask for a million dollars and then sit on your sofa and wait for it to arrive.

If you're doing group rituals, it's important that you like the other members of the group. If there's any form of disharmony, the results are likely to be mixed.

It's natural to have doubts after a ritual. Discard these as soon as you realize you're thinking negatively. Tell yourself that you've put your intent out and it will happen.

The best thing to do after a ritual is to carry on with your everyday life while remaining confident that your intent will manifest.

fourteen

Tarot Rituals

Tarot cards provide knowledge and wisdom in the form of images and symbols. The cards can be used as a spiritual tool, to make contact with your Higher Self, as a means of obtaining guidance and advice, and for meditation and divination purposes.

There are many fanciful theories about the origins of the tarot deck, but the only thing that's known for certain is that the earliest known tarot decks were produced in northern Italy in the mid-fifteenth century.

Apart from its many other uses, the tarot deck can be an extremely useful ritual tool. The deck consists of seventy-eight cards divided into two groups: the major arcana (the greater secrets) and the minor arcana (the lesser secrets). The twenty-two cards of the major arcana symbolize universal themes and the major events in our lives. The fifty-six cards of the minor arcana represent our everyday concerns. They are divided into four suits: cups, wands, pentacles, and swords.

The suit of cups relates to the element of water and symbolizes feelings and emotions.

The suit of wands relates to the element of fire and symbolizes energy, enthusiasm, and creativity.

The suit of pentacles relates to the element of earth and symbolizes security, skill, and financial reward.

The suit of swords relates to the element of air and symbolizes communication, thoughts, and self-expression.

There are hundreds of different tarot decks on the market. If you don't already have a deck, choose one that has pictures on every card, as they are much easier to work with. I have a large collection of tarot decks, but the one I use the most is the Universal Tarot produced by Lo Scarabeo in Italy. This deck is readily available, and it contains illustrations that are simple to interpret and understand.

Purifying Your Cards

Many people buy a deck of tarot cards and immediately start using them. I prefer to gradually become familiar with a new deck before using it for the first time. I start this process by examining each card in turn. I do this even if I've bought a replacement deck for one that I've worn out. I'm constantly surprised with the insights that occur when I do this. This process also imbues the cards with my energy. After I've done this, I conduct a small ritual to purify the cards.

Required: Four gemstones (I use amethyst, bloodstone, lapis lazuli, and tiger's eye), one white candle, salt (either a small bowl containing salt or a solution of salt and water), a small bowl of water, and a silk cloth to wrap your tarot cards in.

1. Place one gemstone in each corner of your working space. Place the white candle at the back of your altar in the center. Place the water on the right-hand side, and the salt on the left-hand side. Place the silk cloth at the edge of your altar on the right-hand side.

2. Place your new deck of tarot cards in the middle of your altar, in front of the candle and between the salt and the bowl of water. Say something along the lines of: "I am now purifying and consecrating you, and welcoming you into my life." Spread the cards, so that at least a small part of each card is visible.

3. Light the candle.

4. Pick up the container of salt and pass it over your cards. Say: "This salt provides you with love and protection from the element of earth." Put the container of salt back on your altar.

5. Pick up the candle and pass it over your cards. Say: "This candle provides you with love and protection from the element of fire." Replace the candle.

6. Pick up the container of water and pass it over your cards. Say: "This water provides you with love and

protection from the element of water." Replace the container of water.

7. Pick up the cards and pass them through the smoke coming from the candle. Say: "This smoke provides you with love and protection from the element of air." Replace the tarot cards on the altar. Spread them slightly to ensure that each card is at least partially visible.

8. Speak to your cards. You can say anything you wish. It might be a simple thanks for the help and advice they're going to give you. It can be a lengthy speech, if you wish. I usually say something along the lines of: "Thank you for entering my life. You are now protected, purified, and energized. I'm going to leave you on my altar for twenty-four hours. When I come back we're going to become closer and closer to each other. Thank you, my friend."

9. Snuff out the candle.

10. If you wish, you can remove the candle, salt, and water. I prefer to leave everything in place until I return the following day.

11. When you return twenty-four hours later pick up the cards, carefully wrap them in the silk cloth, and then remove the other items.

12. Keep the cards with you for about a week, to allow them to become totally familiar with you, and then start using them.

As you can see, this is an extremely simple ritual. I don't cast a circle or perform any invocations. At one time I used joss sticks to provide the smoke for the air element. (I used sage or rosemary.) I found candle smoke works just as well. However, you should use incense if you feel it will help you.

I wrap my tarot cards in a red or dark blue square of silk. Many people choose black as they feel this is the best color to ward off negative energy. You should use any color that appeals to you. At one time, I used a large multicolored handkerchief that was given to me by a close friend. I wouldn't have chosen this normally, but as it was a gift from a friend who had selected it especially for me and my tarot cards, I used it for many years. If your square of silk is large enough, you can also use it as a spread to lay your cards out on.

How to Create a Tarot Card Talisman

A talisman is an object that provides a specific power, energy, and protection to the person who owns or carries it. Talismans are usually made for a specific purpose, and they are always intended to provide some sort of benefit for their owner.

Talismans can be made from almost any material, and they are believed to be most effective when made by their owner. Traditionally, talismans were made of metal, stone, or parchment, but many came in natural forms. Primitive people used objects made from parts of animals as talismans. A shark's tooth or a leopard's claw, for instance, was worn not only for protection, but also to give the wearer some of the qualities of the animal the object originally belonged to.

You can charge almost anything you wish and use it as a talisman. Tarot cards are extremely useful for this, as every card has a meaning and can be charged to attract to you whatever it is you desire.

The first thing to do is to choose a suitable card for whatever your purpose happens to be. If you want courage, for instance, the most obvious card would be Strength. However, other cards might be more suitable for your particular needs. Consequently, you should go through the cards and find the one that resonates best for you.

Here are some possibilities:

The Fool: To recapture feelings of joy and innocence.

The Magician: To gain confidence in your own abilities and worth.

The High Priestess: To develop your psychic and spiritual potential.

The Empress: To make your plans grow and develop. Fruitfulness.

The Emperor: To fully appreciate what you already have. Leadership.

The Hierophant: To progress in a structured environment.

The Lovers: To increase the romantic bond between two people. Friendship. Cooperation.

The Chariot: To focus on a specific goal until success is achieved.

Strength: To develop courage and inner strength.

The Hermit: To search for hidden truths, and to grow in knowledge and wisdom.

The Wheel of Fortune: To attract new and better opportunities.

Justice: To encourage justice and fair play in your dealings with others.

The Hanged Man: To encourage lateral thinking and to appreciate other points of view.

Death: To be able to handle major changes and transformation.

Temperance: To encourage harmony, peace, and reconciliation.

The Devil: To eliminate obsessions, negativity, and addictions.

The Tower: To help handle unexpected changes and disruptions.

The Star: To provide a better future.

The Moon: To handle difficult emotions and stress.

The Sun: To provide happiness, fulfillment, and success. This card can also be used to improve health.

Judgment: To handle karma, and to start progressing again.

The World: To achieve success and accomplishment.

Three of Cups: To attract joy, laughter, and happiness.

Five of Cups: To express your emotions.

Seven of Cups: To enhance existing relationships.

Ten of Cups: To appreciate the beauty of the world.

Queen of Cups: To realize that it's not necessary to always act on your emotions.

Three of Pentacles: To appreciate the contributions of other people.

Six of Pentacles: To realize that the more you give, the more you receive in return.

Seven of Pentacles: To aid and encourage a financial improvement.

Two of Wands: To understand the mysteries of the universe.

Five of Swords: To encourage creativity.

Seven of Swords: To know what you want, and to persevere until it happens.

Knave of Swords: To make new friends.

King of Swords: To appreciate the wisdom that ultimately comes from a hard-won experience.

Once you've chosen a suitable card, you need to perform a divination to make sure that creating this talisman is in your best interests at this time. A good question to ask is: "What will happen if I charge this talisman?"

Assuming you receive a positive answer from your divination, you can design a ritual. As a talisman is an important tool, I'd do a complete ritual that included:

1. Cleaning the area where the ritual will be held.
2. Drawing the circle, and placing the tarot card and other items on your altar.
3. Taking a ritual bath or shower.
4. Performing the Lesser Banishing Ritual of the Pentagram.
5. Charging the tarot card (see the next section).
6. Performing the Lesser Banishing Ritual of the Pentagram.
7. Putting everything away.
8. Recording what happened in your journal.

How to Charge Your Tarot Talisman

There are a number of different ways to charge a talisman.

1. You can expose it to the four elements, using your candle flame, smoke, salt, and water, while asking the four elements to help you charge your talisman.

2. You can ask the goddess to help you. Before performing the ritual, think of a word or short phrase that represents everything your talisman is going to do. Stand outside on a clear night with a waxing moon. Place the tarot card on the palm of your right hand, and hold it in position with your left thumb. The other fingers of the left hand go under the right hand to support it. Gaze upward at the moon and say the word or phrase you created. Start speaking in a quiet voice, and increase the volume and intensity each time you repeat it. After a number of repetitions, you'll suddenly know that it's time to stop. Pause for several seconds, and say the word or phrase one last time in a quiet voice while raising your hands to shoulder height to symbolically offer the tarot card to the moon.

   While still in this position, quietly thank the moon for charging your talisman. Say anything else you wish to say, and then slowly lower your arms and hands.

3. The Kahunas of Hawaii believe that we are made up of three parts. They could be considered to be different aspects of our mind, but the Kahunas visualize them as being in different parts of the body. The "high self," or our spiritual nature, is situated immediately above the head. The "middle self," or our thinking capabilities, is situated in the brain. The "low self," or the feeling, emotional side of our natures, is located in the solar plexus. According to the Kahunas, to achieve a goal, you first have to think about it using the middle self. It then needs to be sent to the low self, where it

is charged with mana, or energy, and then sent to the high self, where it will become a reality. This method is a highly effective way to charge a talisman.

This ritual should be done when the moon is waxing. Have a bath or shower before you start to ritually purify yourself.

Stand with your feet about a foot apart. Rest your talisman on the palm of your right hand and hold it in position with your left thumb. The left fingers support the right hand from below. Close your eyes and take four or five slow, deep breaths through your nose, holding each one for a few seconds before exhaling. With each inhalation feel the life-giving mana entering your body and going deep into your lungs. After four or five breaths pause to sense if your body is full of mana. If it isn't, breathe normally for about thirty seconds, and then take another four or five deep breaths.

Once you feel you're virtually overflowing with mana, sit down in a straight-backed chair. The Kahunas imagined themselves filled to overflowing with water, which is what they used to symbolize mana. Once you feel full to overflowing, visualize a powerful burst of energy erupting from your solar plexus, shooting up your body, and out through the top of your head where it forms a circle of energy immediately above your head. The Kahunas visualize this as a sudden burst of water. I usually think of it as an erupting volcano. The actual visualization you make doesn't matter as long as you know unquestionably that you've sent an offering of life-enhancing mana to your high self.

Now that you've revitalized your high self, it's ready to receive your request. Turn your right hand and clasp your tarot talisman between the palms of your hands as if making a prayer. Think about your need for this talisman, and visualize a picture of this need inside the ball of energy above your head, in your high self. Visualize this for as long as you can. When the picture starts to fade, say your request in a clear, confident, strong voice.

The final stage is to thank your high self for charging your tarot talisman. Pause for several seconds before doing this. When the time feels right, say: "Thank you, high self, for charging my talisman and for granting my request. I am grateful for all of your blessings upon me. Thank you."

Your talisman is now charged.

4. This method can be done at your altar, but the room or sacred space can't be disturbed for several hours after the charging is over. The moon should be waxing, and you need to bathe before you start.

Place the tarot card on your altar. Take a step back and thank the universal life force for protecting and guiding you.

Recite a poem that you enjoy. It needs to be a serious poem, rather than a limerick or piece of doggerel. You might even write your own poem as part of the preparation for this ritual.

Once you've finished your recitation, stare at your talisman for thirty seconds. When you feel ready, speak to it. You might say: "I empower and consecrate you for *(whatever your purpose happens to be)*. I imbue you with all the powers of the universe to enable you to carry out your task, and I thank you in advance for all the energy, power, and comfort that you offer to me." Gaze at your talisman for thirty seconds, and then say "thank you" to it. Spread your arms out wide, look upward, and say "thank you" again.

Leave the room as quietly as you can, and make sure that the room is not used again for several hours. If possible, leave your talisman on the altar until the following morning.

Destroying Your Talisman

The ancient Egyptians believed that the magical properties imbued in a talisman would last forever. This belief is still prevalent today. There'll be times when you don't want your talisman to keep on working indefinitely. Once you've achieved the goal you charged the talisman for, you'll no longer need it. When this occurs, you need to create a small ritual, thanking it for helping you achieve your goal, and to say good-bye.

1. Prepare your sacred space.
2. Place a white candle and your tarot talisman on your altar.
3. Have a bath or shower to purify yourself.

4. Return to your sacred space and light the candle. Stand in front of the candle with the talisman in your cupped hands. Turn to the east and bow. Do the same for south, west, and north, and then turn to face the candle again. Raise your cupped hands to chest level and talk to the talisman. Tell it something along the lines of: "Thank you for helping me achieve my goal. I greatly appreciate all you've done for me. However, you have completed your task and fulfilled your purpose, and now I must let you go. Thank you once again."

5. Hold the talisman as high as you can for a few moments, and then burn it in the flame of the candle. You'll probably experience genuine sorrow as your talisman burns. This is not surprising, as you're effectively saying good-bye to a friend. Watch it burn, and place the ashes in a container in front of the candle.

6. Snuff out the candle. Bow to each of the four quarters again, and leave the circle.

7. Wait at least an hour before disposing of the ashes and tidying up your sacred space.

Tarot and Your Dreams

We all dream, even though some people claim they don't. Most people dream for about two and a half hours every night. Dreams are essential for our health and well-being as they enable us to release emotional thoughts and feelings that might otherwise cause problems.

Usually, our dreams fade quickly as soon as we wake up. It can be a good practice to keep a dream diary beside your bed, so you can write down your dreams before they fade and disappear. A pad of paper or an exercise book is all that's required. If you have a recording device, you might choose to use that.

When you wake up, lie quietly for a few minutes and recall as much of the dream as you can. Once you've done this, sit up and write down everything you remember using as much detail as possible. Don't try to interpret the dream at this stage. That can be done later. Initially, the important part is to record it in as much detail as you can.

If you wake up knowing that you've just had a dream but can't remember it, remain lying in the position you were sleeping in and wait to see what memories come back. There's no need to worry if you can't recall it. If the information was important, you'll dream about it again.

The best time to remember your dreams is when you wake up naturally. For most people this is only possible during the weekend or when they're on vacation. Before falling asleep, tell yourself that you want to remember your dreams in the morning.

Once you've recorded a dream, and had time to analyze it, you can create a ritual using your tarot cards to answer specific questions about the dream. The best questions to ask start with who, what, where, when, why, and how. I like to write the questions down before starting the ritual.

I usually light two white candles that I place on either side of my work surface when performing this ritual. They help me get into the right state of mind before asking any questions. However, the candles are not essential and you can dispense with them, if you wish.

1. Hold your tarot cards in your cupped hands and ask the divine to help you perform the ritual.

2. Sit down and mix your tarot cards while looking at the questions you're going to ask them to answer.

3. Deal out three or four cards and use them to provide insights into your first question. If they don't provide sufficient information, deal out more cards, one at a time, until you have all the details you need. Record your findings in your dream diary.

4. Repeat step two with your other questions.

5. When you've received answers to all your questions, snuff out the candles, and thank the divine for helping you.

I use tarot cards for this ritual, as I find the familiar images comforting and helpful. However, if you're familiar with another divination system, you should use that in preference to the tarot.

Creating a Tarot Card Ritual for a Specific Purpose

No matter what your goal might be, there's a tarot card that will symbolize it. This is the card you'll use in the ritual.

When thinking about the particular ritual you're going to perform, see if you can come up with any unusual, offbeat, or humorous words or actions that you can include.

Anything slightly out of the ordinary will make the ritual more memorable and more effective. This is because you'll think about the unusual or funny aspects of what you've done from time to time, and these thoughts will bring the entire ritual back into your mind.

Some years ago, a friend of mine wanted to start teaching the piano to make extra money to help support her family. Unfortunately, the piano she owned was extremely old, and it looked as if it were more suited to a honky-tonk bar than a teaching studio. She applied to borrow money from her bank, and she was turned down. Rather than despairing or giving up on her goal, she decided to create a ritual to get the money she needed.

She started by writing a letter to the CEO of the bank explaining what she planned to do and how she planned to repay the loan in less than a year. She included the names and contact details of several people who had expressed interest in using her services. She also performed a divination to make sure that what she was intending to do was a good idea.

Before creating a ritual, she recorded herself playing a piece on her old piano. She then went to a music store and tested several pianos that were in her price range, assuming she got the loan. When she found the piano she wanted, she recorded herself playing the same piece on this piano, too. She asked one of the staff members to take a photograph of her playing this piano.

When it was time to perform the ritual, she placed the letter inside an addressed and stamped envelope and put it on her altar. On top of it, she placed the card that she thought related best to her intention of starting a part-time business—the Nine of Pentacles. She placed the photograph of herself playing the piano she wanted in a frame on the right-hand side of her altar. She lit a green candle, which she placed behind the envelope and tarot card. She chose a green candle as this color relates to money.

She acknowledged the four directions by holding her arms out and welcoming each one in turn. She then turned the tarot card facedown and listened to the piece she had recorded on her old piano. She followed this by turning the tarot card face up and listening to the music she'd recorded on the new piano.

Once she'd done this, she picked up the frame containing the photograph and pressed the tarot card against it. "This is what I want," she told the tarot card. "I want that new piano, as it will help me start a new career. I'll be able to work around the activities of my children and earn the extra money we need for my family. Please, please help me."

She picked up the envelope containing the letter she'd written to the bank manager and held it high in her right hand. She picked up the tarot card in her left hand and raised it as high as she could, too. She then started singing the ABBA song "Money, Money, Money" while dancing around her altar. She continued doing this until she felt exhausted.

She finished the ritual by kissing the envelope and thanking the four directions. She snuffed out the candle and immediately drove to the post office to post the letter.

She had intended repeating the ritual every day, but a number of family activities prevented her from doing it.

However, several times every day she remembered how enthusiastically she'd sung the song while dancing around her altar. She was not at all surprised when, a few days later, she received a phone call from her bank asking her to come in and talk to them again about her loan application.

This time she went prepared with a budget, a list of prospective customers, her personal income statements, and some character references. The loan officer gave these only a cursory glance, and told her that he was approving the loan, secured against the piano. He also asked if he could enroll his daughter as a student.

My friend paid off the loan without any problems, and her piano tuition business has continued to grow. She now has a grand piano as well as the one she bought using the bank loan. After a year, she was able to give up her part-time job in a supermarket and become a full-time piano teacher. She credits much of her success on what she calls her "crazy ritual." Interestingly, she has two framed pictures in her music room. One is the photo that was taken in the music store, and the other is the Nine of Pentacles.

While I was writing this, a lady I know told me about a crazy ritual she created to rejuvenate her marriage. She and her husband, who I also know, had been married for thirty-five years. However, the intimacy had gradually faded, and she wasn't sure what to do.

"I had three choices," she told me. "I could accept the situation. That meant I'd stop feeling angry and frustrated all the time. We'd simply grow old together while the relationship slowly crumbled. I could leave the marriage. Owen probably wouldn't be surprised if I told him I no longer loved him and wanted a divorce. It must be obvious that my needs were not being satisfied. Finally, I could change the situation. We were deeply in love at one time. Surely, it was worth putting some time and effort into saving it. I just had to work out how to change things so that both of us were happy."

The first thing my acquaintance did was perform a divination to see if doing something crazy to try to save the marriage would be the best thing for both her and her husband. Once she received a positive response to that, she started thinking of different possibilities.

My friend chose the Lovers card as her "crazy lucky card," and she kept it with her while she weighed the pros and cons of the different things she and her husband could do. She and her husband had led full lives, and she wrote down a lengthy list of crazy things they'd done together over the years. After thinking about these for several days, she made her decision.

On their honeymoon, thirty-five years earlier, they'd spent a night at a resort hotel where there was a great deal of thermal activity. They'd found a small pool of hot water in the river that provided heat and water to the hotel. After bathing in the pool, they'd made love under the stars.

"It was the perfect sacred space," she told me. "It was magical, with steam rising from the pool and the stars up above. I thought we could reenact that night, if only I could find it again."

Her husband showed little interest when she told him that she and a couple of girlfriends were going away for the weekend. With her lucky card inside her purse, the woman drove her friends to the resort and was disappointed to find the hotel and the pools all looked shabby and old.

It didn't take long to find the pool she remembered with such fondness. It didn't look nearly as appealing as it had all those years ago. One of her friends suggested that they come back after dark to have another look. After dinner, they returned and Lorna was relieved to see it was exactly as she remembered it. This was going to be her sacred space.

It took a few weeks to talk her husband into going away for the weekend. He wasn't happy that she refused to tell him where they were going, and he got into the car with bad grace when they set off for the resort.

My friend was disappointed that he said nothing when they arrived at the hotel. It looked as if he didn't remember it. She put this down to the shabby state the hotel was in. She fondled her lucky card and kept quiet until after they'd had dinner.

The husband appeared surprised when she suggested they take a walk. The pond was quiet, and he was stunned when she started to undress. "I'm going to have a swim," she said. "How about you?" She was naked and in the pool before he even started to take off his clothes.

"This brings back memories," he said, once he was in the pool. He cuddled Lorna, and they started talking about their honeymoon all those years ago. When they got out of the pool, it seemed perfectly natural to make love lying on the grass that surrounded the pool.

"It was magic," she told me. "It was as if we'd gone back in time. The grass felt the same, the steam from the pool was the same, and it was a cloudless night, so we could gaze up at the stars. It was the turning point for our marriage, too. I could see that we were destined to grow old together, and I was happy. We had a wonderful weekend, and we've been back there several times since. It's our sacred space, and going back there saved our marriage."

She had thought of several ways to rekindle her husband's interest while they were at the resort, but none of them were necessary. Her "crazy" ritual of taking her husband swimming in a thermal pool was all that was required. She still keeps the Lovers card in her purse.

You can create your own "crazy rituals." Anything that contains movement, fun, laughter, and a strong intention has a special magic about it, and you'll be able to relive it in your mind whenever you wish.

conclusion

A recent study conducted by professor Ted Kaptchuk at Harvard Medical School's Osher Center demonstrated the power of medical ritual on a group of eighty patients suffering from irritable bowel syndrome. Half of the patients received no treatment during the course of the experiment, while the other half were given placebo pills to take twice a day. Usually, patients do not know when they are given placebos, but in this experiment the patients were given bottles of pills that had "placebo" printed on them. They were told that the pills were made from inert substances similar to sugar pills. In addition, the patients were told to take the pills, even if they didn't believe in them, as clinical studies had shown that the placebo effect could cause the mind to help heal the body.

At the end of the three-week trial, the patients taking the placebo pills showed significant improvement over the control group, with almost twice as many of them reporting a satisfactory relief of their symptoms. Even more extraordinary was the finding that they also doubled the average rate of improvement achieved when the most powerful medications available for their condition was used. Professor Kaptchuk reported that "these findings suggest that rather than mere positive thinking, there may be significant benefit to the very performance of medical ritual" (Jha 2010). I've been prescribed pills on occasion, and I hadn't considered taking them at certain times to be a ritual, but of course it is.

Practice your small daily rituals until they become a habit. It's a good idea to perform them at the same time every day, and arrange your daily activities around them. Taking time out for yourself is highly beneficial. It improves your mood and effectiveness, reduces stress, and gives you something to look forward to every day. It's important to nurture yourself, and everyday rituals are a good way to do this.

Create rituals of your own. There is no right or wrong way to do this. You can make your rituals as simple or as elaborate as you wish. It's best to start with simpler rituals, as they can be performed quickly and easily. The preparation and work involved with complicated and involved rituals can be stressful when you're not used to it.

You might consider creating your own circle and inviting like-minded friends to join. This isn't for everyone, as some people prefer performing rituals on their own. You'll need to decide how often you'll meet, how formal or informal the meetings will be, and the purpose or intention of the group. A circle focused on spiritual growth might be a good choice. You'd need a specific goal or intention for each meeting. It's a good idea to have a wand or carved stick for people to hold. The person holding this stick at any given time has the right to speak, and everyone else must listen. The leader of the group (this could be the same person at every meeting or it could change from meeting to meeting) needs to ensure that no one monopolizes the proceedings, and everyone who wants to has a chance to speak.

Dr. Harvey Whitehouse, director of the Institute of Cognitive and Evolutionary Anthropology at the University of Oxford, considers rituals to be "the glue that holds social groups together." He leads a team of anthropologists, archaeologists, economists, historians, and psychologists from twelve universities in the United Kingdom, United States, and Canada who are studying the effects of rituals on humanity, and how they help build up and maintain society and culture (Jones 2013).

In addition to this, I believe all rituals nurture the soul, and consequently are spiritual acts. A simple solo ritual can add enormous meaning and purpose to your life. All rituals are important, even ones that occur spontaneously.

I hope this book has shown you how to use the magic of ritual to effect change in your life. You and I, along with everyone else, have the potential to create whatever it is we most desire. Like everything else, it takes time to master the art of ritual. Be patient. Monitor your results. If you allow them to, rituals will help you create the life you want to live.

Correspondences

In chapter 4, we looked at some of the correspondences relating to the four elements. Many people have written entire books containing lists of magical correspondences, and you'll probably want to purchase at least one of these as you develop your ritual magic skills.

According to Isaac Bonewits, author of *Real Magic*, "the major function of the brain seems to be association." Consequently, it's probably not surprising that anything you name can be associated with something else. Some associations are easy. If I said the word "love," for instance, you could easily come up with a lengthy list of names that relate to love. It's not quite so easy to compile a list of words that relate to the word "ant," but if you spend a minute or two thinking about it, I'm sure you'll come up with a number of associations. Everything is connected to something else, but no one thing is connected to everything else.

Correspondences are links that unite items that might not normally be connected. Magical correspondences are mystical associations that are used to help focus intent and direct energy. Using the right crystal, herb, candle, number, or even magical tool can make a huge difference to the success of your magical rituals. Magical correspondences are sometimes referred to as sympathetic magic, as the energy of one object can be used to influence someone or something that has some form of association with it. There may be an element of like attracting like in prehistoric cave paintings depicting hunting scenes.

Magicians have been using correspondences for thousands of years, but lists of tables of correspondences were first compiled and published by Peter de Abano (1250–1316), Johannes Trithemius (1462–1516), and Heinrich Cornelius Agrippa half a millennium ago. Dr. William Wynn Westcott and S. L. MacGregor Mathers, two of the founders of the Hermetic Order of the Golden Dawn, developed this work considerably in the late nineteenth century. Unfortunately, there is a great deal of disagreement about specific correspondences, and you'll find considerable variations in different books. This is not as bad as it sounds. The best way is to start using the correspondences suggested by one person, and once you've become familiar with them, try the ideas of other authors to see which ones work best for you. In time, you may come up with your own correspondences that relate perfectly for you.

You don't need to limit magical correspondences to your rituals. You can wear clothes and jewelry, for instance, containing colors that relate to your intent. A perfume can have the same effect. You may carry or wear a charm or amulet that relates to your intent. These enable you to work on your goals wherever you happen to be.

Here are some of the more useful correspondences that you can use to help create your own magical rituals.

Colors

Aqua
Zodiac sign: Pisces
Planet: Venus
Day: Friday
Element: Water
Major intent: Aqua is a useful color for any intentions involving compassion, gentleness, and peace of mind.

Black
Zodiac signs: Virgo, Libra, Scorpio, Sagittarius, and Capricorn
Planets: Pluto and Saturn
Days: Saturday and Tuesday
Elements: Earth and water
Major intent: Black absorbs negative energy and should be used only when you feel surrounded by negativity, and can think of no other way to release it.

Black is a useful color for any intentions involving absorbing negative energy, acceptance, anger, authority, banishing negativity, beginnings, binding, challenges, creativity, death, determination, divination, endings, envy, fertility, grief, grounding, justice, karma, knowledge, loss, magic, negativity, patience, persistence, protection, psychic ability, real estate, rebirth, sacrifice, secrets, sleep, spirituality, strength, transformation, truth, and wisdom.

Blue

Zodiac signs: Gemini, Scorpio, Sagittarius, and Aquarius

Planets: Jupiter, Moon, and Neptune

Day: Friday

Element: Water

Major intents: Blue encourages clear thinking and dissipates anger and negativity. You should use blue if your intent relates to honesty, loyalty, and trust.

Blue is a useful color for any intentions involving business, childbirth, communication, dreamwork, emotions, energy, faithfulness, forgiveness, friendship, good fortune, the home, hope, intuition, justice, life, loneliness, the mind, obstacles, pregnancy, prosperity, protection, the psychic world, purification, relationships, sleep, spirituality, travel, truth, willpower, and wisdom.

Brown

Zodiac signs: Gemini, Virgo, Libra, and Capricorn

Planets: Earth, Saturn, and Pluto

Element: Earth

Major intent: Brown can be used for any intent involving endurance, hard work, responsibility, and material success.

Brown is a useful color for any intentions involving agriculture, animals, balance, concentration, courage, endurance, finding lost objects, gardening, grounding, healing, the home, material goods, money, nurture, pets, protection, stability, telepathy, and the truth.

Gold

Zodiac signs: Leo, Virgo, and Sagittarius

Planet: Sun

Day: Sunday

Element: Fire

Major intent: Gold can be used for any intention involving power, prosperity, and worldly success.

Gold is a useful color for any intention involving abundance, beauty, confidence, creativity, divination, friendship, happiness, the god, healing, the home, influence, luxury, masculine energy, money, positivity, power, security, strength, success, understanding, and wealth.

Green

Zodiac signs: Taurus, Gemini, Leo, Virgo, Scorpio, and Aquarius

Planets: Earth, Mercury, and Venus

Days: Thursday and Friday

Elements: Earth and water

Major intent: Green eases troubled situations and provides
determination and persistence. It is a good color if your
intent involves healing or financial improvement.

Green is a useful color for any intentions involving abundance, acceptance, accomplishment, action, agriculture, artistic interests, beauty, change, creativity, energy, family, fertility,
finances, gardening, generosity, grounding, growth, herbs, the
home, life, longevity, luck, marriage, money, music, nurture,
partnerships, peace, physical and emotional healing, prosperity, protection, relationships, and success.

Indigo
Zodiac signs: Capricorn, Aquarius, and Pisces

Planets: Jupiter, Neptune, Saturn, and Uranus

Days: Thursday, Friday, and Saturday

Element: Water

Major intent: Indigo resolves family tensions, and enhances
love and happiness. It's a good color to use if your intent
involves home and family matters.

Indigo is a useful color for any intentions involving ambition, clarity, clairvoyance, divination, fear, guidance, home
and family, honesty, inner peace, karma, marriage, meditation, psychic ability, purification, rebirth, spirituality, and the
truth.

Orange
Zodiac signs: Taurus, Gemini, Cancer, Leo, Scorpio, and Sagittarius

Planets: Mars, Mercury, Moon, and Sun

Days: Sunday, Tuesday, and Wednesday

Element: Fire

Major intent: Orange is a good color if your intent involves creativity, a happy future, or resolving female sexual problems.

Orange is a useful color for any intentions involving abundance, adaptability, affection, alertness, ambition, beginnings, business, celebration, confidence, creativity, discipline, energy, freedom, goals, goodness, healing, the home, justice, kindness, legal matters, luck, mental acumen, money, opportunity, pleasure, positivity, power, reconciliation, relationships, stimulation, strength, travel, and well-being.

Pink

Zodiac signs: Aries, Taurus, Gemini, Cancer, Virgo, and Libra

Planet: Venus

Days: Friday and Sunday

Elements: Air and fire

Major intent: Pink is the perfect color to use if your intent relates to close relationships or nurturing yourself on an emotional level.

Pink is a useful color for any intentions involving acceptance, affection, attraction, beauty, children, compassion, emotions, exercise, femininity, friendship, happiness, kindness, love, marriage, maturity, nurturing, partnerships, passion, sensuality, stress, warmth, and worry.

Purple

Zodiac signs: Virgo and Sagittarius

Planet: Mercury

Days: Wednesday and Thursday

Element: Water

Major intent: Purple is the perfect color to choose if your intent relates to spirituality or anything involving helping humanity as a whole. It can also be used to relieve any tension between friends and colleagues.

Purple is a useful color for any intentions involving accomplishment, ambition, astrology, authority, emotions, enlightenment, government, growth, healing, the home, independence, influence, intellect, luck, manifestation, power, protection, psychic matters, spirituality, transformation, truth, wisdom, and writing.

Red

Zodiac signs: Aries, Taurus, Gemini, Leo, Scorpio, Sagittarius, Capricorn, and Pisces

Planet: Mars

Day: Tuesday

Elements: Air and fire

Major intent: Red is a powerful color that can be used for any intent involving courage, strength, sexual matters, and major life changes. It is useful for resolving male sexual problems.

Red is a useful color for any intentions involving action, ambition, assertiveness, business, conflicts, courage, creativity, desire, drive, energy, health, joy, love, loyalty, mechanical objects, mercy, motivation, passion, protection, romance, sexuality, sports, strength, willpower, and wisdom.

Silver

Zodiac signs: Gemini, Cancer, and Aquarius

Planet: Moon

Days: Monday and Wednesday

Elements: Air and water

Major intent: Silver is a harmonizing and balancing color that relates to the moon. It can be used for any intent involving change, learning, and femininity.

Silver is a useful color for any intentions involving awareness, beginnings, challenges, creativity, divination, dreams, fame, the goddess, healing, insight, intuition, money, power, protection, psychic awareness, purification, spirituality, stability, and success.

Violet

Zodiac signs: Gemini, Virgo, Libra, Capricorn, Aquarius, and Pisces

Planet: Mercury

Day: Wednesday

Element: Water

Major intent: Violet is a good choice if your intent involves inspiration, intuition, and spirituality.

Violet is a useful color for any intentions involving clarity, creativity, focus, the goddess, healing, higher self, insight, introspection, intuition, peace, power, protection, psychic ability, purification, sensitivity, spirituality, transformation, and wisdom.

White

Zodiac signs: Aries, Gemini, Cancer, Virgo, Libra, and Capricorn

Planets: Earth, Moon, and Venus

Days: Sunday, Monday, Friday, and Saturday

Elements: Air, earth, fire, and water

Major intent: White cleanses, clarifies, heals, and purifies. It is a good choice for any intent involving these.

White is a useful color for all intentions, but especially those involving balance, beginnings, calmness, clarity, concentration, confidence, consecration, divination, enlightenment, grounding, guidance, happiness, healing, hope, initiation, innocence, optimism, peace, protection, psychic perception, purity, spirituality, strength, truth, and willpower.

Yellow

Zodiac signs: Aries, Gemini, Cancer, Leo, Virgo, Libra, Sagittarius, and Aquarius

Planets: Mercury and Sun

Days: Sunday and Wednesday

Elements: Air and fire

Major intent: Yellow relates to communication, learning, and the intellect. It also attracts similarly minded friends and creates a positive environment. Consequently, it's a good choice if your intent involves communication and friendship.

Yellow is a useful color for any intention involving awareness, change, clarity, communication, creativity, dedication, dreamwork, friendship, grounding, happiness, the home, inspiration, intellect, intuition, knowledge, learning, pleasure, positivity, protection, psychic ability, stimulation, travel, warmth, and wisdom.

Days of the Week

Sunday

Zodiac sign: Leo

Planet: Sun

Number: 1

Colors: Amber, gold, orange, yellow, and white

Plants: Angelica, bay, carnation, chamomile, frankincense, marigold, mistletoe, rosemary, St. John's wort, and sunflower

Gemstones: Amber, carnelian, clear quartz, diamond, sunstone, tiger's eye, yellow topaz

Deities: Apollo, Baal, Brigid, Cernunnos, Helios, Lugh, Sekhamet, and Sol

Sunday is a good day for any rituals involving ambition, attraction, authority, children, career, confidence, creativity, entertainment, fame, friendship, fun, goal-setting, health, justice, leadership, men's mysteries, money, personal growth, power, promotion, prosperity, protection, self-worth, spirituality, success, transformation, and wealth.

Monday

Zodiac sign: Cancer

Planet: Moon

Numbers: 2 and 9

Colors: Blue, gray, pearl, silver, and white

Plants: Chamomile, jasmine, lily, moonflower, poppy, sandalwood, violet, and willow

Gemstones: Aquamarine, chalcedony, clear quartz, emerald, moonstone, mother-of-pearl, pearl, and sapphire

Deities: Artemis, Athena, Bast, Cerridwen, Diana, Isis, Juno, Luna, and Selene

Monday is a good day for any rituals involving children, clairvoyance, creativity, divination, dreams, emotions, family, fertility, health, home, illusion, intuition, love, magic, meditation, pets, prophecy, protections, the psychic world, psychology, sincerity, spirituality, wisdom, and women's mysteries.

Tuesday

Zodiac signs: Aries and Scorpio

Planet: Mars

Number: 5

Colors: Black, orange, pink, and red

Plants: Allspice, basil, camellia, clematis, dragon's blood, garlic, ginger, mustard, pepper, snapdragon, and thistle

Gemstones: Bloodstone, emerald, garnet, ruby, and topaz

Deities: Ares, Horus, Mars, Oghma, Tiwaz, and Tyr

Tuesday is a good day for any rituals involving action, assertiveness, authority, business, career, courage, discipline, energy, healing, integrity, men, new beginnings, partnerships, physicality, protection, purification, self-esteem, sexuality, standing up for yourself, strength, truth, and ultimate success.

Wednesday

Zodiac signs: Gemini and Virgo

Planet: Mercury

Number: 3

Colors: Magenta, orange, purple, silver, violet, and yellow

Plants: Almond, caraway, clover, dill, fennel, jasmine, lavender, lemongrass, and lily of the valley

Gemstones: Agate, amethyst, aventurine, citrine, lodestone, opal, ruby, sapphire, and turquoise

Deities: Anubis, Hecate, Hermes, Mercury, and Odin

Wednesday is a good day for any ritual involving artistic endeavors, business, chance, communication, contracts, courage, creativity, education, fears, fortune, insight, knowledge, languages, legal matters, loss, luck, mental stimulation, money, self-expression, self-improvement, study, travel, wisdom, and writing.

Thursday

Zodiac signs: Sagittarius and Pisces

Planet: Jupiter

Numbers: 4 and 8

Colors: Blue, green, and purple (and metallic colors)

Plants: Borage, cinnamon, cinquefoil, clove, dill, honeysuckle, mint, nutmeg, and patchouli

Gemstones: Amethyst, aventurine, carnelian, cat's eye, garnet, malachite, peridot, sapphire, and turquoise

Deities: Juno, Jupiter, Neptune, Nuada, Thor, and Zeus

Thursday is a good day for any ritual involving abundance, business, charity, expansion, finances, growth, healing, honor, legal matters, luck, philosophy, prosperity, protection, publishing, relationships, religion, study, success, travel, wealth, and well-being.

Friday

Zodiac signs: Libra and Taurus

Planet: Venus

Numbers: 6 and 9

Colors: Aqua, blue, green, pink, and white

Plants: Apple, apricot, catnip, feverfew, foxglove, geranium, heather, hyacinth, lilac, magnolia, rose, thyme, and violet

Gemstones: Alexandrite, cat's eye, celenite, chalcedony, chrysoberyl, clear quartz, emerald, rose quartz, and ruby

Deities: Aphrodite, Bacchus, Brighid, Freya, Frigg, Hathor, Venus, and Vesta

Friday is a good day for any ritual involving affection, balance, beauty, emotions, entertainment, fertility, friendship, gardening, happiness, harmony, love, magic, partnerships, passion, peace, pleasure, pregnancy, relationships, romance, sexuality, soul mates, and wisdom.

Saturday

Zodiac signs: Aquarius and Capricorn

Planet: Saturn

Number: 7

Colors: Black, indigo, purple, red, and white

Plants: Amaranth, beet, belladonna, comfrey, hellebore, ivy, mimosa, morning glory, mullein, slippery elm, and wolfsbane

Gemstones: Amethyst, black tourmaline, diamond, hematite, jet, labradorite, obsidian, onyx, and turquoise

Deities: Chronos, Cybele, Demeter, Hecate, Loki, Osiris, Pluto, Saturnus, and Set

Saturday is a good day for any rituals involving accomplishment, ambition, attraction, banishing, cleansing, confidence, creativity, finances, friendship, goals, healing, karma, leadership, material gain, patience, perseverance, personal growth, property, protection, spirituality, stability, strength, success, truth, and wisdom. Saturday is a good day for eliminating negative emotions and feelings.

Gemstones

Agate
Zodiac signs: Cancer, Virgo, Libra, and Capricorn

Planet: Moon

Element: Earth

God: Aesculapius

People used to believe that taking an agate to bed with you cured insomnia and provided enjoyable dreams. Agate is useful in any ritual involving calmness, communication, diversity, friendship, luck, optimism, success, and the truth.

Alexandrite
Zodiac signs: Gemini, Scorpio, and Pisces

Planet: Venus

Elements: Earth and water

Goddesses: Juno

Alexandrite was discovered in Russia in 1830, and is named after Tsar Alexander II. It is useful for any rituals involving balance, beginnings, confidence, intuition, limitations, money, nervousness, relationships, sexuality, and trust.

Amethyst

Zodiac signs: Virgo, Sagittarius, Capricorn, Aquarius, and Pisces

Planets: Jupiter, Neptune, and Pluto

Element: Water

Gods: Bacchus and Dionysius

Goddesses: Diana, Justitia, and Venus

Amethyst means "not drunk," as until comparatively recently people believed it kept people sober no matter how much alcohol they consumed. Amethyst is useful in any rituals involving concentration, dreams, enjoyment, friendship, healing, inner peace, negativity, and stability.

Aquamarine

Zodiac signs: Aries, Gemini, Virgo, Libra, Scorpio, Aquarius, and Pisces

Planets: Moon and Neptune

Element: Water

God: Mars

Because of its name, aquamarine was believed to protect sailors and their ships. Aquamarine is useful in any rituals involving clarity, concentration, fear, healing, protection, psychic ability, purification, relationships, strength, and travel.

Aventurine

Zodiac signs: Capricorn and Pisces

Planets: Earth and Neptune

Elements: Earth and water

Gods: Thor and Zeus

Goddess: Juno

Because it's green in color, gamblers in the United States often carry it to attract good luck and money. Aventurine is useful in any rituals involving abundance, changes, confidence, experience, happiness, learning, luck, money, opportunities, and protection.

Beryl

Zodiac signs: Cancer, Libra, Scorpio, and Capricorn

Planets: Mars, Moon, and Neptune

Element: Water

Gods: Neptune and Poseidon

Goddess: Tiamat

In ancient Greece, beryl was a popular stone for divination, healing, and meditation. Beryl is useful for any rituals involving acceptance, divination, energy, enthusiasm, friendship, healing, love, psychic ability, relationships, and travel.

Bloodstone (aka Heliotrope)

Zodiac signs: Aries, Libra, Scorpio, Capricorn, and Pisces

Planets: Earth and Mars

Element: Fire

Goddess: Badb

The dark red spots on bloodstone were believed to have come from the blood of Jesus when he was crucified. Bloodstone is useful for any rituals involving abundance, anger, healing, love, luck, meditation, pregnancy, relationships, spirituality, and success.

Blue Lace Agate

Zodiac signs: Virgo, Libra, and Pisces

Planets: Venus, Uranus, and Neptune

Elements: Air and water

Goddesses: Juno

Blue lace agate helps you to listen carefully and to speak your mind in important conversations. It's useful for any ritual involving calmness, communication, confidence, healing, opportunities, relationships, spirituality, stress, and the truth.

Calcite

Zodiac sign: Cancer

Planets: Moon and Venus

Element: Water

Calcite is a common stone that can be found in a wide variety of forms and colors. It is useful in any ritual involving ambition, awareness, goals, money, protection, and stability.

Carnelian

Zodiac signs: Aries, Taurus, Cancer, Leo, Virgo, Scorpio, and Capricorn

Planets: Earth, Mercury, Saturn, Sun, and Venus

Element: Fire

Goddess: Isis

In the Islamic world, it was believed that carnelian could fulfill any desire. Apparently, Mohammed wore a carnelian ring to ensure a blessed afterlife (Stern 1946). Carnelian is useful in any rituals involving communication, confidence, courage, healing, negativity, sexuality, success, travel, and wisdom.

Chrysoprase

Zodiac signs: Taurus and Libra

Planets: Earth and Venus

Element: Earth

Goddess: Vesta

In the Middle Ages, thieves believed that holding a piece of chrysoprase in the mouth would make them invisible. Chrysoprase is useful for any rituals involving anxiety, compassion, emotions, healing, money, protection, sorrow, and wisdom.

Citrine

Zodiac signs: Aries, Gemini, Leo, Libra, and Scorpio

Planets: Earth, Mars, Mercury, and Sun

Element: Fire

Goddess: Ishtar

As natural citrine is comparatively rare, most citrine is created by heating low-quality amethyst to about 900 degrees Fahrenheit. At this temperature it turns golden in color. Citrine is useful in any rituals involving abundance, creativity, finances, growth, relationships, sleep, spiritual guidance, and vitality.

Clear Quartz

Zodiac signs: Aries, Gemini, Cancer, Capricorn, and Aquarius

Planets: Moon, Sun, and Uranus

Element: Air

Goddess: Hecate

Quartz is by far the most popular New Age stone, and can be used for almost any purpose. It is useful in any rituals involving clarity, emotions, fertility, finances, goals, healing, the home, meditation, self-improvement, spirituality, support, and wisdom.

Diamond

Zodiac signs: Aries, Taurus, Leo, Virgo, Libra, and Pisces

Planets: Mars, Sun, and Venus

Element: Fire

God: Dagda (sometimes spelled Daghdha)

Goddess: Danu

Diamond is the hardest natural material to be found in nature. Diamond is useful in any rituals involving beauty, business, confidence, family, leadership, love, power, protection, psychic ability, reconciliation, relationships, and wealth.

Emerald

Zodiac signs: Aries, Taurus, Gemini, Cancer, Virgo, Libra, and Sagittarius

Planets: Jupiter and Venus

Element: Earth

Gods: Hermes, Mercury, and Vishnu

Goddess: Venus

Emerald was traditionally the stone of Venus, and she wore it every Friday on her holy day. Hermes Trismegistus is said to have written the Words of Creation on the famous

Emerald Tablet. Emerald is useful in any rituals involving creativity, emotions, love, luck, protection, psychic ability, travel, and wealth.

Garnet
Zodiac signs: Aries, Leo, Virgo, Capricorn, and Aquarius
Planets: Mars and Pluto
Element: Fire
Goddess: Badb

It used to be believed that garnets could not be stolen, as they'd cause the thief great bad luck until the stone was returned to its owner. Garnet is useful in any ritual involving balance, compassion, dreams, emotions, fertility, friendship, loyalty, luck, power, and protection.

Hematite
Zodiac signs: Aries, Taurus, Capricorn, and Aquarius
Planets: Earth and Mars
Elements: Earth and fire
Gods: Loki and Osiris

People used to believe hematite bled, as it produced a red fluid when ground or cut in water. Hematite is useful in any ritual involving anxiety, grounding, happiness, meditation, negativity, protection, purification, and willpower.

Jade
Zodiac signs: Aries, Taurus, Gemini, Virgo, Libra, Aquarius, and Pisces
Planets: Neptune and Venus
Elements: Earth and water

God: Buddha

Goddesses: Coatlicue, Guanyin, and Maat

Jade is the sacred stone of China. It's useful in any ritual involving abundance, desire, dreams, gambling, luck, money, motivation, prosperity, protection, and wisdom.

Jasper

Zodiac signs: Leo, Libra, and Pisces

Planets: Mercury and Venus

Element: Earth

Goddess: Isis

Jasper has been considered a healing stone for thousands of years. It's useful for any ritual involving compassion, concentration, encouragement, grounding, healing, negativity, positivity, pregnancy, protection, and strength.

Lapis Lazuli

Zodiac signs: Aries, Taurus, Virgo, Libra, Sagittarius, and Capricorn

Planets: Neptune and Venus

Element: Water

Goddesses: Isis, Justitia, Nut, and Venus

Lapis lazuli was sacred to the ancient Egyptian goddess Isis. It is useful in any rituals involving addiction, anger, calmness, communication, grounding, healing, intuition, love, protection, psychic ability, spirituality, the truth, and wisdom.

Magnetite (aka Lodestone)

Zodiac signs: Gemini and Virgo

Planets: Jupiter and Neptune

Element: Water

Because it's magnetic, magnetite used to be worn by prostitutes to attract customers. Magnetite is useful in any rituals involving healing, luck, relationships, sexuality, stress, and support.

Malachite

Zodiac signs: Taurus, Libra, Scorpio, and Capricorn

Planets: Venus and Saturn

Element: Earth

God: Njord

Goddess: Juno

In ancient Rome, malachite was used to protect babies and young children from harm. Malachite is useful in any rituals involving communication, emotions, gardening, luck, money, protection, self-improvement, spirituality, and success.

Moonstone

Zodiac signs: Gemini, Cancer, Libra, Scorpio, and Pisces

Planet: Moon

Element: Water

Goddesses: Diana, Hecate, Isis, Luna, and Selene

In the Middle Ages, people believed the moonstone could predict the future, especially when the moon was waning. Moonstone is useful in any ritual involving clairvoyance, compassion, contemplation, dreams, fertility, intuition, meditation, menopause, psychic ability, sensitivity, stress, and wisdom.

Obsidian

Zodiac signs: Scorpio, Sagittarius, and Capricorn

Planets: Pluto and Saturn

Element: Fire

Gods: Lugh and Tezcatlipoca

Goddesses: The Morrigan and Pele

Obsidian was revered throughout the ancient world, and in Mexico it was called the divine stone. Obsidian is useful in any rituals involving anger, divination, grief, grounding, guilt, protection, shame, spirituality, and support.

Opal

Zodiac signs: Taurus, Cancer, Virgo, Libra, Scorpio, Sagittarius, and Pisces

Planets: Saturn, Neptune, and Venus

Element: Water

God: Cupid

The ancient Greeks and Romans believed opals enabled people to see well into the future. Opals are useful in any ritual involving adaptability, emotions, intuition, love, luck, obstacles, protection, psychic ability, stress, and wisdom.

Peridot

Zodiac signs: Capricorn, Leo, and Virgo

Planets: Mercury, Sun, and Venus

Elements: Earth and fire

Goddesses: Banba, Brighid, and Pele

Some people claim that peridot was used as a healing stone in Atlantis (Stein 1987). Peridot is useful in any rituals involving calm, energy, gratitude, happiness, healing, jealousy, love, prophecy, protection, stress, transition, travel, and wisdom.

Rose Quartz

Zodiac signs: Taurus, Cancer, and Libra

Planet: Venus

Element: Water

God: Aengus

Goddess: Venus

Rose quartz is useful in any rituals involving comfort, compassion, contentment, grief, joy, kindness, loss, love, nurturing, peace, romance, support, and unity.

Ruby

Zodiac signs: Aries, Leo, and Sagittarius

Planets: Mars and Sun

Element: Fire

Gods: Buddha and Krishna

Goddess: The Morrigan

Ruby was believed to be able to store heat, and to bring cold water to a boil (Kunz 1913). Ruby is useful in any rituals involving action, creativity, enthusiasm, inner strength, intuition, love, passion, sexuality, spirituality, and wisdom.

Sapphire

Zodiac signs: Taurus, Gemini, Cancer, Leo, Virgo, Libra, Aquarius, and Pisces

Planets: Moon, Neptune, Saturn, and Venus

Element: Water

Gods: Aengus, Apollo, and Lugh

Goddesses: Hecate and Justitia

In medieval Europe, people believed that people who wore sapphire would gain the gift of prophecy. Sapphire is useful in any rituals involving clarity, confidence, contemplation, emotions, leadership, meditation, self-esteem, understanding, and wisdom.

Sodalite

Zodiac sign: Sagittarius

Planet: Jupiter

Element: Earth

Sodalite was first discovered in Greenland in 1906. It is useful in any ritual involving dreams, emotions, endurance, grounding, intuition, meditation, psychic ability, stress, and wisdom.

Turquoise

Zodiac signs: Gemini and Sagittarius

Planets: Jupiter and Mercury

Element: Air

Goddesses: Chalchiuhtlicue, Guanyin, Hathor, and Maat

It was believed that if you fell down while wearing a turquoise, you would not break any limbs. When Emperor Charles V of France asked his jester about this, the jester's reply was: "If you should happen to fall from a high tower whilst you were wearing a turquoise on your finger, the turquoise would remain unbroken" (Kunz 1913). Turquoise is useful in any rituals involving clarity, communication, inspiration, intuition, love, luck, manifestation, spirituality, truth, and wisdom.

Herbs

Angelica

Zodiac signs: Aries and Leo

Planet: Sun

Element: Fire

Goddess: Venus

Angel: Michael

Angelica is an extremely powerful herb of protection that banishes negativity while attracting positivity. It's useful in rituals involving acceptance, attraction, consecration, divination, friendship, growth, harmony, luck, peace, spirituality, stability, strength, support, and ultimate success.

Basil

Zodiac signs: Aries and Scorpio

Planets: Mars, Pluto, and Venus

Element: Fire

Gods: Ares, Jupiter, Krishna, Loki, Mars, Obatala, Seth, and Vishnu

Goddesses: Aradia and Lakshmi

Basil can be strewn on floors to banish negativity, and it can also be carried or worn to attract money. Basil is useful in rituals involving assertiveness, business, concentration, finances, healing, the home, luck, money, power, protection, psychic ability, purification, relationships, success, and sympathy.

Bergamot

Zodiac signs: Aries, Leo, and Sagittarius

Planets: Mercury, Moon, and Venus

Element: Air

Gods: Hermes, Mercury, and Shango

Goddess: Fortuna

Bergamot is a powerful herb that attracts success. It's useful in rituals involving awareness, balance, confidence, courage, emotions, focus, love, money, positivity, prosperity, success, and wealth.

Catnip

Zodiac signs: Cancer, Libra, and Pisces

Planet: Venus

Element: Water

Goddesses: Bast and Sekhmet

Cats adore catnip, so it's not surprising that it's sacred to Bast. Many people grow catnip in their gardens to attract good luck. Catnip is useful in any ritual involving animals, courage, dreams, fertility, happiness, the home, love, luck, psychic potential, strength, and stress.

Chamomile

Zodiac signs: Cancer and Leo

Planet: Sun

Element: Water

Gods: Cernunnos, Mercury, and Ra

Chamomile reduces stress and helps people get to sleep. Washing your hands with chamomile is believed to increase your luck in gambling. Many people believe that bathing in chamomile attracts love. Chamomile is useful in rituals involving anxiety, attraction, beauty, calm, communication, dreams, happiness, healing, introspection, intuition, justice, love, manifestation, patience, stress, and support.

Cinquefoil
Zodiac sign: Taurus
Planets: Jupiter and Saturn
Elements: Earth and fire
God: Jupiter

Cinquefoil is a good general-purpose herb that can be used for almost anything. The five points of the leaf symbolize health, love, money, power, and wisdom. It can be used in all rituals, especially those involving business, confidence, divination, dreams, eloquence, the home, love, memory, protection, romance, and travel.

Clover
Zodiac sign: Gemini
Planet: Mercury
Element: Air
Gods: Gwydion and Rowan
Goddess: Artemis

Clover can be carried as an amulet to provide faithfulness, intelligence, luck, and protection. Clover is useful in rituals involving acceptance, the community, dream working, fidelity, friendship, healing, intuition, love, luck, protection, and wealth.

Columbine
Zodiac signs: Taurus and Libra
Planet: Venus

Element: Water

Goddess: Freya

Columbine provides courage in difficult and stressful situations. It can be grown in the garden to attract fairies. Columbine is useful in rituals involving anxiety, childbirth, love, pregnancy, purification, and stress.

Coriander

Zodiac signs: Aries and Virgo

Planet: Mars

Element: Fire

God: Tyr

Coriander helps relieve troubled relationships, and it is frequently used in charms to attract love. Coriander is useful in any ritual involving headaches, healing, love, lust, peace, and protection.

Dill

Zodiac signs: Gemini, Cancer, Leo, Virgo, and Scorpio

Planet: Mercury

Element: Fire

God: Mercury

Goddess: Brighid

Dill is used in charms for luck and protection. Dill is useful in any rituals involving desire, energy, the home, love, luck, lust, money, prosperity, protection, purification, stress, willpower, and wisdom.

Fennel

Zodiac signs: Aries, Gemini, and Virgo

Planet: Mercury

Element: Fire

Gods: Adonis, Dionysius, and Prometheus

Fennel is believed to increase longevity and to ward off negativity. It's useful in any rituals involving communication, courage, energy, fertility, finances, healing, the home, longevity, protection, and virility.

Garlic

Zodiac sign: Aries

Planet: Mars

Element: Fire

God: Mars

Goddess: Hecate

Garlic can be hung in the home to enhance family relationships. Garlic is useful in any rituals involving aggression, banishing, communication, emotions, fear, healing, the home, justice, purification, stimulation, and worry.

Hawthorn

Zodiac sign: Aries

Planet: Mars

Element: Fire

God: Hymen

Goddess: Flora

Hawthorn has been used in the bedroom to encourage chastity in unmarried people. Interestingly, it's also used in weddings to encourage fertility. Hawthorn is useful in any rituals that involve career, celibacy, employment, fertility, happiness, money, averting negativity, protection, and rebirth.

Heather

Zodiac signs: Taurus and Scorpio

Planet: Venus

Element: Water

Goddess: Venus

Heather can be hung in the home to attract peace. It can also be carried or worn to provide protection. Heather is useful in any rituals involving adaptability, authority, confidence, dreams, generosity, growth, healing, the home, knowledge, longevity, love, luck, peace, protection, psychic perception, spirituality, and trust.

Honeysuckle

Zodiac signs: Aries, Taurus, Cancer, Leo, Virgo, Scorpio, Sagittarius, Capricorn, and Pisces

Planets: Jupiter, Mars, and Mercury

Element: Earth

Goddesses: Luna and Selene

It's said that your psychic powers will improve if you rub crushed honeysuckle flowers into your forehead. Honeysuckle is useful for any ritual involving abundance, affection, balance, confidence, creativity, divination, education, friendship, happiness, inspiration, intuition, memory, peace of mind, prosperity, protection, psychic ability, stress, and well-being.

Hyssop

Zodiac signs: Gemini and Virgo

Planets: Jupiter and Mercury

Element: Air

God: Obatala

Hyssop is the most popular, and arguably the best, purification herb. It eliminates negativity and stress when hung in the home. Hyssop is useful in any rituals involving affection, authority, cleansing, concentration, confidence, consecration, negativity, protection, purification, psychic ability, strength, and stress.

Lavender

Zodiac signs: Gemini, Leo, Virgo, Aquarius, and Pisces

Planet: Mercury

Element: Air

Goddesses: Aradia and Hecate

Lavender heals sadness and depression. It also enhances sleep and brings harmony into the home. Lavender is useful in any rituals involving anxiety, courage, dreams, healing, intuition, loneliness, love, luck, manifestation, peace, purification, relationships, romance, stability, stress, support, and worry.

Marjoram

Zodiac signs: Aries, Gemini, Virgo, and Libra

Planet: Mercury

Element: Air

Marjoram can be placed in the corners of different rooms in the home to provide protection and to eliminate negativity. It's also frequently used to attract a suitable partner. Marjoram is useful in any rituals involving attraction, family, happiness, the home, love, peace of mind, protection, psychic acumen, purification, sleep, stress, and warmth.

Mugwort

Zodiac signs: Taurus, Gemini, Cancer, Libra, and Sagittarius

Planet: Venus

Elements: Air and earth

Goddesses: Artemis, Diana, Isis, and Lakshmi

Mugwort can be placed around any divination or ritual tools to increase their power. Placed near or under the bed, mugwort promotes astral travel and prophetic dreams. Mugwort can be used in any ritual involving authority, community, divination, dreams, fertility, health, joy, love, protection, psychic ability, purification, sleep, and visions.

Parsley

Zodiac sign: Gemini

Planet: Mercury

Element: Air

Goddess: Persephone

Parsley protects the home and attracts good luck. Traditionally, it was mixed with jasmine and carried in the person's shoes to increase his or her popularity with the opposite sex. Parsley can be used in any rituals involving calmness, fertility, friendship, learning, luck, prosperity, protection, romance, strength, vitality, and well-being.

Pennyroyal
Zodiac sign: Libra

Planet: Mars

Element: Fire

Goddess: Demeter

Pennyroyal can be worn to increase business success and to eliminate negativity. Pennyroyal is useful in any rituals involving anxiety, business, healing, the home, money, negativity, protection, strength, stress, and worry.

Rosemary
Zodiac signs: Aries, Leo, Virgo, Sagittarius, and Aquarius

Planets: Mercury, Moon, and Sun

Element: Fire

Goddesses: Ganesha and Hathor

Rosemary can be worn or carried to improve memory retention. Rosemary is useful for any ritual involving attraction, comfort, concentration, confidence, dreams, emotions, empowerment, family, love, loyalty, luck, marriage, memory, nightmares, protection, psychic potential, sleep, willpower, and youth.

Sage

Zodiac signs: Taurus, Sagittarius, Aquarius, and Pisces

Planets: Jupiter and Mercury

Elements: Air and earth

God: Chiron

Sage can be carried to promote physical, mental, emotional, and spiritual health. It removes all negative energies. Sage is useful in any ritual involving balance, business, career, concentration, confidence, fear, fertility, grounding, guidance, healing, knowledge, longevity, love, marriage, protection, spirituality, strength, and wisdom.

St. John's Wort

Zodiac signs: Leo and Sagittarius

Planet: Sun

Element: Fire

St. John's wort can be placed under a pillow to induce prophetic, romantic dreams. It can also be carried to provide confidence, courage, and wisdom. St. John's wort is useful in all rituals involving confidence, courage, dreams, energy, fear, fertility, freedom, happiness, healing, luck, money, power, prosperity, purification, spirituality, and strength.

Thyme

Zodiac signs: Aries, Taurus, Libra, and Capricorn

Planet: Venus

Elements: Air and water

Goddesses: Ceres and Demeter

A sprig of thyme can be worn to provide confidence, courage, and strength. It can also help the grieving process. Thyme is used in any ritual involving awareness, confidence, courage, grief, happiness, healing, the home, inner growth, honesty, luck, money, protection, psychic ability, sleep, strength, stress, and well-being.

Vervain

Zodiac signs: Gemini, Sagittarius, and Capricorn

Planet: Venus

Elements: Air, earth, and fire

Gods: Hermes, Jupiter, Mars, Thor, and Zeus

Goddesses: Aphrodite, Aradia, Artemis, Cerridwen, Hecate, Isis, Juno, and Venus

Vervain can be kept in the home to provide peace of mind, encourage wealth, and provide protection. Vervain is useful in any ritual involving anxiety, dreams, grounding, healing, learning, love, money, protection, psychic ability, purification, sleep, wealth, and youth.

Intent

Abundance

Planet: Jupiter

Colors: Green and orange

Number: 8

Gemstones: Agate, aventurine, bloodstone, citrine, jade, malachite, peridot, and quartz

Gods: Cernunnos, Jupiter, and Zeus

Goddesses: Anu, Bast, Cerridwen, Demeter, Isis, Lakshmi, Rhea, and Rhiannon

Acceptance
Planet: Earth
Element: Air
Colors: Green and pink
Gemstone: Quartz
Herbs: Blueberry, clover, and iris
God: Anansi
Goddess: Atalanta

Alcoholism (to Break)
Planet: Earth
Element: Air
Colors: Brown and green
Gemstone: Amethyst
Herbs: Cypress, patchouli, sage, and lavender

Anger
Planet: Mars
Element: Fire
Colors: Black and red
Gemstones: Agate, amethyst, and emerald
Herbs: Gorse, peony, and wormwood
God: Aegir, Mars, and Nergal
Goddesses: Durga, Hera, Nemesis, and Sekhmet

Attraction
Planets: Sun, Venus, and waxing Moon
Colors: Gold, orange, pink, and yellow

Gemstones: Hematite, lodestone, and tourmaline

Herbs: Cinnamon, frangipani, ginseng, jasmine, marjoram, patchouli, and wisteria

Gods: Aengus and Krishna

Business (for Success)

Planets: Mercury and Jupiter

Element: Earth

Color: Green

Gemstones: Bloodstone, green tourmaline, and malachite

Herbs: Cinnamon and patchouli

Gods: Cernunnos, Hermes, Lugh, Mercury, and Osiris

Goddesses: Demeter, Hera, Juno, and Minerva

Children (to Protect)

Planet: Moon

Elements: Fire and water

Colors: Red and blue

Gemstones: Agate, amber, and lapis lazuli

Herbs: Caraway, hyssop, lavender, and motherwort

Goddesses: Artemis, Brigid, Hathor, Hecate, Isis, and Sekhmet

Courage (to Attract)

Planet: Mars

Element: Fire

Color: Red

Gemstones: Agate, amethyst, bloodstone, garnet, lapis lazuli, quartz crystal, and ruby

Herbs: Allspice, basil, dragon's blood, lavender, and thyme

Gods: Atlas, Mars, Mithras, and Tyr

Goddesses: Athena, Ishtar, and Isis

Drug Addiction (to Break)

Element: Water

Color: Blue

Gemstones: Amethyst, jade, and rose quartz

Herbs: Lavender, peppermint, rose, and sage

Employment (to Find Satisfying Work)

Planets: Sun and Jupiter

Element: Earth

Colors: Green and yellow

Gemstones: Bloodstone, peridot, tiger's eye, and topaz

Herbs: Allspice, basil, dill, heliotrope, and sage

Gods: Bladud, Janus, and Vulcan

Goddess: Inanna

Friendship (to Attract)

Planets: Jupiter, Sun, and Venus

Element: Water

Color: Pink

Gemstones: Amethyst, chrysoprase, moss agate, rose quartz, tourmaline, and turquoise

Herbs: Angelica, chamomile, coriander, and lemon balm

God: Eros and Thor

Guilt (to Let Go Of)

Element: Air

Color: Yellow

Gemstones: Aquamarine, calcite, pearl, and rose quartz

Herbs: Anise, rosemary, and slippery elm

Gods: Dionysius and Enki

Goddess: Ate

Health (and Healing)

Planets: Jupiter and Sun

Elements: Water and fire

Color: Blue

Gemstones: Carnelian, hematite, peridot, and turquoise

Herbs: Cinnamon, eucalyptus, peppermint, and sage

Home (to Attract)

Planet: Saturn

Element: Earth

Colors: Green and brown

Gemstones: Apache tear, hematite, and obsidian

Herbs: Fern, patchouli, and vervain

Jealousy (to Release)

Element: Earth

Color: Blue

Gemstones: Amethyst and rose quartz

Herbs: Cardamon, coriander, lemon, and rosemary

Love (to Attract)
Planet: Venus

Element: Water

Color: Pink

Gemstones: Amethyst, jade, moonstone, and turquoise

Herbs: Basil, lavender, rosemary, and thyme

Money (to Attract)
Planets: Jupiter and Sun

Element: Earth

Color: Green

Gemstones: Aventurine, bloodstone, jade, peridot, and tiger's eye

Herbs: Basil, clove, dill, nutmeg, and sage

Protection
Planets: Mars and Sun

Element: Fire

Colors: Red and white

Gemstones: Carnelian, garnet, and quartz crystal

Herbs: Basil, bay, dill, juniper, and sage

Relationship (to Strengthen)
Planet: Moon

Element: Water

Colors: Pink and red

Gemstones: Rose quartz and pink tourmaline

Herbs: Basil, chamomile, lavender, and rose

Stress (to Ease)

Planet: Mars

Element: Water

Color: Blue

Gemstones: Amethyst, calcite, kunzite, malachite, and soda-lite

Herbs: Cumin, lavender, and pennyroyal

Numbers

One

Zodiac signs: Aries and Leo

Planets: Mercury and Sun

Day: Sunday

Colors: Gold, orange, white, and yellow

Element: Fire

Gods: Apollo, Freyr, and Ptah

Goddesses: Aphrodite, Diana, and Vesta

One relates to action, ambition, assertiveness, business, courage, creativity, finances, independence, leadership, luck, new beginnings, optimism, success, and willpower.

Two

Zodiac signs: Taurus and Gemini

Planets: Mars and Moon

Day: Monday

Colors: Dark blue, green, and white

Element: Water

Gods: Loki and Saturn

Goddesses: Ceres, Frigg, Rhea, and Venus

Two relates to adaptability, balance, cooperation, diplomacy, friendship, gentleness, imagination, intuition, love, patience, romance, and support.

Three

Zodiac sign: Gemini

Planets: Jupiter, Mars, Moon, and Saturn

Day: Wednesday

Colors: Green, purple, and violet

Element: Fire

God: Pluto

Goddesses: Hecate and Modron

Three relates to action, beauty, communication, creativity, friendship, harmony, healing, joy, luck, manifestation, the mind, pleasure, protection, psychic acumen, and success.

Four

Zodiac sign: Leo

Planets: Earth, Jupiter, Mercury, and Uranus

Day: Thursday

Colors: Blue, brown, and gray

Element: Earth

Gods: Jupiter, Odin, and Zeus

Four relates to accomplishment, attraction, business, compassion, conscientiousness, desire, discipline, hard work, harmony, limitations, loyalty, money, restrictions, stability, system and order, and well-being.

Five

Zodiac signs: Taurus and Leo

Planets: Jupiter, Mars, Mercury, and Venus

Day: Tuesday

Colors: Gray, red, silver, and white

Element: Air

Gods: Dionysius, Mars, and Thor

Goddesses: Cerridwen, Ishtar, Kali, and Minerva

Five relates to action, change, communication, desire, freedom, inspiration, intellect, love, opportunities, optimism, sensuality, spirituality, travel, and variety.

Six

Zodiac signs: Gemini and Virgo

Planets: Sun and Venus

Day: Friday

Colors: Blue, gold, and pink

Element: Earth

Gods: Bacchus and Hermes

Goddesses: Athena and Freya

Six relates to affection, balance, comfort, community service, family, friendship, happiness, harmony, the home, kindness, love, luck, peace, relationships, spirituality, sympathy, and wisdom.

Seven

Zodiac sign: Libra

Planets: Neptune, Saturn, and Venus

Day: Saturday

Colors: Green, purple, and white

Element: Water

God: Mithras

Goddesses: Athena, Frigg, Idunn, and Minerva

Seven relates to clairvoyance, divination, faith, fear, fertility, healing, imagination, introspection, intuition, knowledge, psychic ability, secrets, spirituality, and wisdom.

Eight

Zodiac signs: Leo and Scorpio

Planets: Mercury and Saturn

Day: Thursday

Colors: Brown, orange, and purple

Element: Earth

God: Mercury

Goddesses: Cybele, Gaia, Hera, and Venus

Eight relates to abundance, accomplishment, ambition, authority, business, discipline, justice, karma, money, patience, power, prosperity, stability, and success.

Nine

Zodiac signs: Virgo, Scorpio, and Sagittarius

Planets: Mars and Moon

Days: Monday and Friday

Colors: Pink, red, silver, and white

Element: Fire

Gods: Odin and Shiva

Goddesses: Aine, Ariadne, Hecate, Hel, Juno, Luna, Rhiannon, and Selene

Nine relates to accomplishment, compassion, completion, courage, emotions, endings, generosity, healing, loss, love, the mind, psychic acumen, sympathy, and wisdom.

bibliography

Agrippa, Heinrich Cornelius. *Three Books of Occult Philosophy.* Translated by James Freake, edited and annotated by Donald Tyson. St. Paul, MN: Llewellyn Publications, 1993.

Bonewits, Isaac. *Real Magic.* Rev. ed. York Beach, ME: Samuel Weiser, 1989. Originally published in 1971.

Castenada, Carlos. *The Active Side of Infinity.* New York: HarperCollins, 1999.

Cicero, Chic, and Sandra Tabatha Cicero. *The Essential Golden Dawn: An Introduction to High Magic.* St. Paul, MN: Llewellyn Publications, 2003.

Crowley, Aleister. *Magick in Theory and Practice.* Paris: Lecram Press, 1929. Republished as *Magick, Book 4 Parts I-IV* by York Beach, ME: Samuel Weiser, Inc., 1997. This book is also available online at several sites, including: http://www.sacred-texts.com/oto.aba/aba.htm.

Farr, Florence, quoted in Mary Greer, *Women of the Golden Dawn: Rebels and Priestesses.* Rochester, VT: Park Street Press, 1995.

Fortune, Dion. *Psychic Self-Defense.* New York: Samuel Weiser, Inc., 1970. Originally published 1930 by Rider and Company, London.

Gino, Francesca, and Michael I. Norton. "Why Rituals Work: There are Real Benefits to Rituals, Religious or Otherwise." *Scientific American* (May 14, 2013). http://www.scientificamerican.com/article/why-rituals-work/.

Halverson, Heidi Grant. "New Research: Rituals Make Us Value Things More." *Harvard Business Review* (December 12, 2013). http://hbr.org/2013/12/new-research-rituals-make-us-value-things-more/.

Jaffé, Aniela. "Symbolism in the Visual Arts." *Man and His Symbols.* Edited by Carl G. Jung. London: Arkana Books, 1990.

Jahn, R. G., and Brenda J. Dunne. *Margins of Reality: The Role of Consciousness in the Physical World.* New York: Harcourt, Brace and Jovanovich, 1987.

Jahn, R. G., et al. "Correlations of Random Binary Sequences with Prestated Operator Intention: A Review of a 12-year Program." *Journal of Scientific Exploration.*

Tiburon, CA: The Society for Scientific Exploration, 1997.

James, William. *The Varieties of Religious Experience*. London: Longmans, Green and Company, 1902.

Jarrett, Christian. "Rituals Bring Comfort Even for Non-Believers." *The British Psychological Society Research Digest* (March 18, 2013). http://digest.bps.org.uk/2013/03/rituals-bring-comfort-even-for-non.html.

Jha, Alok. "Placebo Effect Works Even if Patients Know They're Getting a Sham Drug." *The Guardian* (December 22, 2010). http://www.guardian.co.uk/science/2010/dec/22/placebo-effect-patients-sham-drug.

Jones, Dan. "Social Evolution: The Ritual Animal." *Nature* 493 (Jan. 24, 2013): 470–472. doi:10.1038/493470a.

Jung, Carl G. *Memories, Dreams, Reflections*. London: Collins and Routledge and Kegan Paul, 1963.

Kempis, Thomas à. *The Imitation of Christ*. Translated by Aloysius Croft and Harold Bolton. Milwaukee, WI: Bruce Publishing Company, 1940.

King, Martin Luther, Jr. "Loving Your Enemies." *The Class of Nonviolence*, prepared by Colman McCarthy of the Center for Teaching Peace. Accessed June 10, 2015. http://salsa.net/peace/conv/8weekconv4-2.html.

Kunz, George Frederick. *The Curious Lore of Precious Stones*. Philadelphia: J. B. Lippincott Company, 1913.

Merton, Thomas. *The Seven Storey Mountain*. New York: Harcourt Brace, 1948.

Plato. *Timaeus*. Translated by H. D. P. Lee. Harmondsworth, UK: Penguin Books Limited, 1965.

Poloma, Margaret, and George Gallup. *Varieties of Prayer.* Harrisburg, PA: Trinity Press International, 1991.

Radin, Dean. *Entangled Minds.* New York: Pocket Books, 2006.

Radin, Dean, and Roger Nelson. "Evidence for Consciousness-related Anomalies in Random Physical Systems." *Foundations of Physics.* Springer Science-Business Media, 1989.

Richardson, Alan. *Aleister Crowley and Dion Fortune.* Woodbury, MN: Llewellyn Publications, 2009.

Rinpoche, Sogyal. *The Tibetan Book of Living and Dying.* New York: HarperCollins, 1992.

Schlitz, M. "Intentionality in Healing: Mapping the Integration of Body, Mind and Spirit." *Alternative Therapies in Health and Medicine.* Mendota Heights, MN: Alternative Therapies in Health and Medicine, 1995.

Schlitz, Marilyn, and William Braud. "Distant Intentionality and Healing: Assessing the Evidence." *Alternative Therapies in Health and Medicine* 3, no. 6 (1997).

Stein, Diane. *The Women's Book of Healing.* St. Paul, MN: Llewellyn Publications, 1987.

Stern, Max. *Gems: Facts, Fantasies, Superstitions, Legends.* New York: Max Stern and Company, 1946.

Webster, Richard. *Omens, Oghams and Oracles.* St. Paul, MN: Llewellyn Publications, 1995.

suggested reading

Ashcroft-Nowicki, Dolores. *The Ritual Magic Workbook: A Practical Course of Self-Initiation*. London: The Aquarian Press, 1986.

Beck, Renee, and Sydney Barbara Metrick. *The Art of Ritual*. Berkeley, CA: Celestial Arts, 1990.

Bell, Catherine. *Ritual: Perspectives and Dimensions*. Oxford, UK: Oxford University Press, 1997.

Biziou, Barbara. *The Joy of Ritual: Spiritual Recipes to Celebrate Milestones, Ease Transitions, and Make Every Day Sacred*. New York: Golden Books, 1999.

Cicero, Chic, and Sandra Tabatha Cicero. *Tarot Talismans: Invoke the Angels of the Tarot.* Woodbury, MN: Llewellyn Publications, 2006.

Cunningham, Nancy Brady. *I am Woman by Rite: A Book of Women's Rituals.* York Beach, ME: Samuel Weiser, Inc., 1995.

Currey, Mason. *Daily Rituals: How Artists Work.* New York: Alfred A. Knopf, 2013.

Davies, Douglas J. *Death, Ritual and Belief.* London: Cassell and Company, 1997.

Greer, Mary G. *The Essence of Magic: Tarot, Ritual, and Aromatherapy.* North Hollywood, CA: Newcastle Publishing Company, 1993.

Hawkins, David R. *Reality, Spirituality, and Modern Man.* Toronto: Axial Publishing Company, 2008.

Holland, Eileen. *Holland's Grimoire of Magickal Correspondences.* Franklin Lakes, NY: New Page Books, 2006.

Hope, Murry. *The Psychology of Ritual.* Longmead, UK: Element Books Limited, 1988.

Knuth, Bruce G. *Gems in Myth, Legend and Lore.* Thornton, CO: Jewelers Press, 1999.

Kunz, George Frederick. *The Curious Lore of Precious Stones.* Philadelphia: J. B. Lippincott Company, 1913.

Kynes, Sandra. *Llewellyn's Complete Book of Correspondences.* Woodbury, MN: Llewellyn Publications, 2013.

Lembo, Margaret Ann. *The Essential Guide to Crystals, Minerals and Stones.* Woodbury, MN: Llewellyn Worldwide, 2013.

Linn, Denise. *Sacred Legacies: Healing Your Past and Creating a Positive Future.* New York: The Ballantine Publishing Group, 1999.

McRae-McMahon, Dorothy. *Rituals for Life, Love & Loss.* Paddington, Australia: Jane Curry Publishing, 2003.

Mégemont, Florence. *The Metaphysical Book of Gems and Crystals.* Rochester, VT: Healing Arts Press, 2008.

Moore, Thomas. *Care for the Soul: Guide for Cultivating Depth and Sacredness in Everyday Life.* New York: HarperCollins, 1992.

Moorey, Teresa, and Jane Brideson. *Wheel of the Year: Myth and Magic Through the Seasons.* London: Hodder & Stoughton, 1997.

Picucci, Michael. *Ritual as Resource: Energy for Vibrant Living.* Berkeley, CA: North Atlantic Books, 2005.

Regardie, Israel. *The Golden Dawn.* Sixth edition. St. Paul, MN: Llewellyn Publications, 2000. First published 1971.

Roséan, Lexa. *The Encyclopedia of Magickal Ingredients.* New York: Paraview Pocket Books, 2005.

Somé, Malidoma Patrice. *Ritual: Power, Healing and Community.* Portland, OR: Swan Raven & Company, 1993.

St. Aubyn, Lorna. *Rituals for Everyday Living.* London: Judy Piatkus (Publishers), 1994.

Walker, Barbara G. *The Book of Sacred Stones: Fact and Fallacy in the Crystal World.* San Francisco: HarperSanFrancisco, 1989.

Webster, Richard. *Amulets & Talismans for Beginners.* St. Paul, MN: Llewellyn Publications, 2004.

————. *Color Magic for Beginners.* Woodbury, MN: Llewellyn Publications, 2006.

————. *Encyclopedia of Angels.* Woodbury, MN: Llewellyn Publications, 2009.

————. *Prayer for Beginners.* Woodbury, MN: Llewellyn Publications, 2009.

————. *Write Your Own Magic.* Woodbury, MN: Llewellyn Publications, 2001.

Weschcke, Carl Llewellyn, and J. H. Slate. *Clairvoyance for Psychic Empowerment.* Woodbury, MN: Llewellyn Publications, 2013.

Westcott, W. Wynn. *Numbers: Their Occult Power and Mystic Virtues.* London: Theosophical Publishing House Ltd., 1974. First published 1890.

Williams, Lynn. *Rituals for an Enchanted Life.* London: Rider, 2002.

To Write to the Author

If you wish to contact the author or would like more information about this book, please write to the author in care of Llewellyn Worldwide Ltd., and we will forward your request. Both the author and publisher appreciate hearing from you and learning of your enjoyment of this book and how it has helped you. Llewellyn Worldwide Ltd. cannot guarantee that every letter written to the author can be answered, but all will be forwarded. Please write to:

Richard Webster
℅ Llewellyn Worldwide
2143 Wooddale Drive
Woodbury, MN 55125-2989

Please enclose a self-addressed stamped envelope for reply, or $1.00 to cover costs. If outside the USA, enclose an international postal reply coupon.